To Toniand Rebecca
May the Stars and their people
guide and Protect you!
Peace and Light
Robert Stail
2008

OUT OF THE STARS

A Message from
Extraterrestrial Intelligence

BY

Robert Short

ISBN 0-7414-1504-6

Front cover by David E. Caywood

Published by:

PUBLISHING.COM

519 West Lancaster Avenue
Haverford, PA 19041-1413
Info@buybooksontheweb.com
www.buybooksontheweb.com
Toll-free (877) BUY BOOK
Local Phone (610) 520-2500
Fax (610) 519-0261

Printed in the United States of America

Printed on Recycled Paper

Published May 2003

TABLE OF CONTENTS

Dedication

This book is dedicated to the memory of such individuals as George W. Van Tassel, Eva Van Tassel, Daniel W. Fry, Daniel Boone, Orfeo Angelucci, George Hunt "RIC" Williamson, and many others who served in the capacity of those who helped to shape and inspire the author of this book down through the early years of UFODOM.

My gratefulness also extends to others such as William Cox, who often allowed my writings to appear in his publication *Pyramid Guide*. Then there is Mr. "UFO" Timothy Beckley, who through his publications made my work and my UFO experiences better known to the world and to those who have continued to study this still mysterious subject called Unidentified Flying Objects.

I would also be remiss if I should overlook my keen interest in the study of prophets and prophecy, more particularly, statements transcribed by Native Americans, such as Hopi, and the very early Mayan prophet Chil'lam Balaam. I am more than grateful to the Sainted Mother of the great world teacher Jesus The Christ, or Mary, who has appeared to many persons around the world and left Her words of inspiration and prophecy. And lastly, to the great seer Nostradamus, who left his legacy of visions of our future.

Acknowledgements

In recognizing my sincere thanks to those who have always been supportive and have over the years offered to help in whatever way possible, I would first offer my deep gratitude to my mother, Delia, for believing in me and accepting my UFO experiences without question. She has always been a spiritual inspiration. Even when this book did not appear possible, she would not allow me to give up. I would also give my heartfelt thanks to my wife, Shirley, who has worked right along with me. Shirley has experienced many UFO appearances, which she has faithfully transcribed, along with other work elsewhere in these pages. She also continues to inspire and believe in the purpose for this book.

There are also those close associates, such as John and Robbin O'Connor, who have been steadfast in lending their strength and love, as well as volunteering to help in many ways for which I am deeply grateful. I would also like to offer my deep appreciation to Brad and Sherry Steiger for their continued friendship, and for Brad's kindness in his Preface to this book.

Lastly, though words are inadequate to express my inner spiritual feelings, I leave my loving thanks and embrace my two friends, Landi Mellas and David Caywood. Their encouragement, love, and hours of labor, together with editing and artwork, have helped in the vision that this book might reach out to touch others throughout this home we call Earth.

-the author

Foreword

I was first exposed to UFO contactee literature in the 1950s with the works of George Adamski and a wide variety of individuals who claimed to have spoken to extraterrestrial intelligences, from Buck Nelson to Andy the Mystic Barber. By 1967, I had become intrigued by the increasing number of men and women who were claiming such communication, and I began a serious study of those individuals who claimed to receive messages, advice, or instruction from the occupants of spaceships.

In my opinion, discounting the more obvious accounts of those men and women who claimed to have visited other planets and boasted of being feted by extraterrestrial royalty, those contactees who emphasized spiritual teachings from Space Intelligences were in the process of creating a blend of science and religion that might form a theology more applicable to contemporary humankind.

The more philosophical among our species have insisted for centuries that life must have meaning. If, as contact with extraterrestrial or other-dimensional intelligences would seem to suggest, we are not alone in the universe, then life does have meaning, for humankind thereby becomes part of a larger community of intelligences.

During the course of my early investigations I met an amiable, yet serious-minded, contactee named Bob Short. What set Bob apart from so many others who claimed to receive messages from Space Intelligences was his ability to discuss the entire UFO mystery and its many facets in an informed manner. This, and his wonderful sense of humor. He was not so self-involved with his messages from Space Intelligences that he could not laugh at himself and some of the incredible situations in which he sometimes found himself.

As destiny would reveal, I soon discovered that the woman who would become my life-research and writing partner, Sherry Hansen, also knew and liked Bob and his wife Shirley, both pastors in the Blue Rose Ministry, in Cornville, Arizona. The four of us have since spent many a delightful evening over dinner in a Chinese restaurant, from Phoenix to Los Angeles.

And now Bob has written a book, *Out of the Stars*, and I am delighted to state that the volume offers the same kind of balanced approach to the contactee enigma that Bob displays in person. Bob explores his relationship with an "extraterrestrial source" by taking the reader through an examination of UFOs in mythology, prophecy, and the history of our species on this planet. Although he openly states that he is a "channel" who relinquishes his physical body in order for "Space Intelligence" to speak through him, Bob also refers to this ability as being "extrasensory," thereby not dogmatically demanding that everyone must agree that his channeled communications necessarily derive from an alien hovering above him in a space ship.

Bob offers advice on how others might develop their sensitivity through such techniques as meditation and allow their spiritual selves to make contact with these intelligences, who might very well be the Heavenly Hosts referred to in the Bible and in other ancient texts. Perhaps, as he suggests, the Heavenly Hosts are very much alive and well and continuing to communicate their teachings and messages to those earthlings sensitive enough to receive them.

Out of the Stars is a book filled with information, inspiration, and inquiry regarding the mystery of the UFO contactee. Perhaps after you have read this fascinating work, you may agree with Bob Short and many other serious-minded men and women that someone has been communicating certain universal truths to us ever since we became human. Certain receptors to this "cosmic broadcast," that is, prophets, revelators, and contactees, have been tuning into these frequencies for centuries, because, for some as yet indeterminate reason, they have been able to receive the channels with greater clarity than their more distracted brothers and sisters. Thank you, Bob, for paying attention!

Brad Steiger
Co-author with Sherry Hansen Steiger of
UFOs Are Here! and many other books
on UFOs and the paranormal.

Introduction

The following information has been developed through and by the extrasensory abilities of Reverend Robert Short, who began his work around 1952 while living in California. He is well documented and is what some refer to as a "UFO contactee and channel." He and his family have all undergone either UFO second, third, or fourth-type encounters; several witnessed by other individuals who were present when they took place. Rev. Short has in his possession affidavits documenting these experiences, as well as those expressing gratefulness to his extraterrestrial sources for their assistance in time of need. Within this book, these extraterrestrial *sources* will also be referred to as *Space Intelligence*.

Although it is expected that some may express skepticism at these experiences or the information that appears here, Rev. Short asks only that the reader keep an open mind as to this type of occurrence and the information he has obtained from this extraterrestrial *Space Intelligence*. His extraterrestrial *sources* state that they are, at present, in another parallel universe and parallel solar system, which is in another time zone or dimension. These particular beings are humanoid and appear as solidly physical, looking very much like our own people on earth. The beings state that they have also established bases (mostly underground) on several of our own nearby planets, as well as satellites on the fringe of our solar system. These bases are all open to members of what the *Space Intelligence* refer to as the *Solar Confederation*.

It is hoped that what you are about to read will not only stimulate your thinking, but will be a catalyst for further research and investigation into the field of UFOs and *Extraterrestrial Intelligence*.

About the Author

Cornville, Arizona resident Robert Short and his wife Shirley, both ordained ministers, have maintained the Blue Rose Ministry since 1970. Their work involves contacting *Extraterrestrial Intelligence*, with Robert functioning as a "channel" and sending the recorded messages to people all over the world. A *channel* is defined as one who relinquishes their body in order for *another intelligence* to communicate through them. Besides his "not so ordinary" ability as a channel, Robert considers himself a regular, everyday person. In his own words:

I was born in 1929 in Sioux City, Iowa, where my father was an executive with W. Swift & Co. When I was five, we moved to Los Angeles where my father worked as a salesman and later a Hollywood agent. As a child, I loved all kinds of music. I fooled around with drums for awhile, attended Hollywood High School with a lot of show people, and then entered the Navy.

My family was not overly religious, nor did they show an overt interest in metaphysical concepts, but even as a child, I believed visitors from another world would come here from space. I felt their arrival would be the greatest event to happen on earth.

After a stint in the Navy, I became interested in UFOs upon hearing of Kenneth Arnold's sightings near Mount Rainier in 1947. Around 1951, this interest took me to Winslow, Arizona, where I began working with George 'Ric' Williamson, and also a gentleman by the name of Lyman Streeter, who claimed to have contacted *Extraterrestrial Intelligence* on his ham radio. When Streeter first started receiving messages, he thought his leg was being pulled, but it proved to be no hoax. Many times during my association with these two men, UFOs hovered over where we were receiving messages. They (*Space Intelligence*) would even answer questions we hadn't asked! We began to contemplate the possibility of bypassing the ham radio altogether and using direct mental telepathy in our communication with the *Space Intelligence*. However, our efforts to explore this possibility were hampered when in 1952 the government closed our operation. Their explanation given for this action was that we did not have proper legal grounds for "extraterrestrial" or "alien" contacts. Because of this, I eventually left Winslow, disappointed at the mindset of those "authorities" who sought to limit our understanding of the *Extraterrestrial Intelligence* and their presence on earth.

Although disappointed, I was not about to give up. One night after arriving back in the San Fernando Valley, I took a flashlight and attempted to signal any UFO that might be hovering in the blackness of space. To my astonishment, some half-dozen UFOs streaked across the sky, their mysterious appearance reinforcing my determination and intense desire to communicate with them. Just how I would accomplish this communication was uncertain, as my previous thwarted efforts at *alien* contact continued to weigh heavily in my memory. However, as is usually the case in my contact with extraterrestrials, I didn't have long to wait for an opportunity.

THE VAULTS OF HEAVEN

Gazing outward into the great expanse of the oceans of space,
I am as a giant reaching out to touch the very vaults of heaven.
I will loose the sweet influence of the Pleiades,
Unbuckle the belt of Orion,
Pluck the harp of Lyra, loose the arrows of Sagittarius,
And walk among the gods of Ursa Majorus.
Perhaps I would be as one of these gods,
As I gaze outward into the heavens,
Identifying the greatness of the cosmic sea.

Therefore, I am never alone!
My world, this beautiful earth,
Is but a grain of sand upon the beaches of the oceans of space.
Those whom we refer to as *space beings*
In their chariots of fire have come down,
Reaching out to me with a great heart.
Their love and peace bid me to join them,
In the great endeavors that stretch before me.

My task may appear as though a great burden,
Yet it rests lightly upon my shoulders.
For it is that which has been appointed me
By the Masters and Elders of the Tribunal and Council.
It might also appear as I walk the avenues of the earth,
That I am alone,
But then I remember that I am surrounded by the many others
Of the same philosophy and field of thought.

I have come to know,
That I am beyond that which is just flesh and bone.
It is this recognition that shakes the vaults of heaven loose
To rain its potential upon me.
I am never left without guidance or direction,
For sufficient is the present day given unto me
To carry out my tasks.
This is what I have been seeking in life,
To progress with my potential, talents and abilities.

I am but a child of earth,
Who sings forth the songs of heaven.
The tones reach my ears and ring forth like a bell within me,
To bring about joy and raise my spirit.
Those whom we term the angelic Cherubim and Seraphim
Bear me upon their wings,
When I would dash my foot against a stone,
Or sink into the depths of negativity.
Their brilliance lifts my pathway,
And I walk proudly upon the surface
That seemingly stretches endlessly before me.

As a child of light, a child of the earth,
I grasp the hand of those from other worlds
Who so willingly give of their benefit, peace and blessings.
For soon, the true name of earth will be called Terra,
Replacing that which has been Saros or Shan,
Repetitive Affliction.
Earth will venture forth, taking its true place among the heavens,
And her children shall reap the pouring forth of enlightenment
From those whose wisdom surpasses all understanding.
A great adventure lies just ahead,
If we would but follow the footsteps.

CHAPTER ONE
GIANT ROCK

Automatic Writing

It was not long after this incident of UFOs streaking across the sky that someone made the fateful suggestion that I try automatic writing. Hesitant at first, I finally took their suggestion, setting up a large artist's pad and holding my hand over it. In the beginning, all I got were swirls. But then something incredible happened. *They* began writing. The writing came so fast that I would feed the paper in with my left hand and immediately feed it out again like an assembly line. An extraterrestrial calling himself *Jon-al* seemed to be my main contact, although another entity would sporadically come through with information. Being a discerning person, I studied the writings carefully. They were intelligent; the messages portraying concepts of higher learning and spiritual truths. Surprisingly during these automatic writing sessions, my arm never grew tired, although I sometimes held it over the paper for an hour. Then, during one of the sessions, the extraterrestrials communicated a message to me.

WE WANT YOU TO GO TO THE BIG ROCK IN THE DESERT IF YOU WISH TO LEARN MORE OF THE TRUTH ABOUT US. My excitement grew as I read the words *they* had written.

"Please show me how to get there," I said. I waited patiently, holding my hand over the paper, but was given no further word. *Why was I not getting anything?* I wondered. *Were these extraterrestrials playing mind games with me?* Somewhat frustrated now at their perceived lack of interest in giving me directions, I put paper and pencil to rest. I would soon discover, though, just how much preparation was actually taking place on their part, and that *synchronicity*, not *coincidence*, is at the core of my involvement with extraterrestrials…

The Man Under the Rock

It was sometime later that my mother learned of a woman who had been to a place near Twenty Nine Palms, California, where "a man underneath the 'big rock' talked to *space people.*" That's all I needed to hear. That same evening, I got into my little Hudson Terraplane coupe and left North Hollywood with some food, water and blankets. *I'm heading out toward Twenty Nine Palms,* I mentally informed my unseen ET contacts. *If this is what you meant during our automatic writing session, then show me how to get there!*

I wound up in the town of Joshua Tree, California. Stopping at a service station, I called to the attendant. "Say, could you tell me where I can find this 'big rock' out here?" He seemed amused at my question, as if he were thinking, *He wants rocks? We've got nothing but rocks!* "Yeah! Take your pick. They're all around you," he called back.

Opening my map, I saw no "big rock" in the Twenty Nine Palms area. "OK, guys, if you're *really* telling me this, can *you* show me how to get there?" I again asked my ET guides. But still I heard only silence. *Just great!* I thought. *Another roadblock on the extraterrestrial highway of life.* Pulling out of the station, I drove five blocks east.

TURN LEFT! a voice shouted in my head. Startled, I quickly swung the car left onto a paved road. Where had the voice come from? My rational mind did not want to believe what I had just heard. "Where do I go now?" I questioned cautiously. Again there was only silence. Heading straight into the desert, I soon came to a fork in the road. *Now what?* I wondered.

TAKE THE ROAD TO THE RIGHT, spoke the voice again. Although I could not see who was speaking to me, by now it was clear that I was being guided by someone, or something.

Following directions, I took the right fork, bouncing along a bumpy, rock-strewn roadway. A light was barely visible in the distance. As I approached, it turned out to be a

2

huge boulder with a windsock and a light on the top. There was no one around. A sign on a nearby building read, *COME ON IN.*

The hour was late. Getting out of the car to stretch my legs, I decided to have some of the food that I had brought with me. The stillness of the night was broken only by the rustling of waxed paper as I unwrapped a sandwich. *What was I doing here anyway?* The slightest shiver crawled up my spine. Perhaps I was just fooling myself and this whole thing would end up a wild goose chase. Swallowing the last bite, I stared into the darkness. The sad howl of a lone coyote echoed in the distance. In a moment, I got back in the car and crawled under the blankets. I would find some gas in the morning and be on my way. Sleep came quickly.

I had every intention of leaving as soon as I awoke the next morning. Rubbing the sleep from my eyes, I scanned my surroundings. Everything looked different in the daylight. I was about to start the car when my curiosity got the best of me. I would first explore the nearby building.

"Good morning. How are you?" A large, rawboned woman greeted me as I walked through the door.

"Oh, fine...fine," I stated.

"What'll you have?"

"What do you mean?"

"Aren't you going to have any breakfast?" she inquired.

"Well, yeah, sure!" My stomach growled. I was hungry.

"What would you like? We have ham and eggs; bacon and eggs; eggs, toast and coffee."

This was so weird! Here I was in the middle of *nowhere* and there's a restaurant!

The woman took my order. As I sat drinking my coffee and waiting for my breakfast, another man walked through the door. She greeted him, poured his coffee, and went back to frying the bacon.

"By the way," I spoke up. "Do you know where I could find a place called the 'Big Rock in the Desert?'"

"I might," the woman said, quite to the point. "It's called Giant Rock, and you're there."

"You're kidding!"

"Why would I do that?" she said, grinning.

I could hardly believe my ears. "Nobody's going to believe that I was *led* to find this place," I told her.

"If you weren't meant to find it, you wouldn't have," she stated. "But obviously since you *have* found it, you're supposed to be here."

"Do you know about this man that talks to...um...you know...flying saucers?" I knew she must have thought I was crazy. I continued anyway. "You know...these things that fly about..."

"You mean S*pace Intelligence?*"
"Yeah, that's it!"

At that moment, I had no idea that I was talking to George Van Tassel's first wife, Eva, a real pioneer with a big heart, and a most wonderful lady. She told me that her husband, George, the man who had entered earlier, was sitting at a bench having his coffee. I walked over to him.

"Mr. Van Tassel?"

The man looked up from the rim of his coffee cup. He had the appearance of a business executive; his Dutch background gave him a crisp, matter-of-fact attitude.

"Mr. Van Tassel, I have some writings outside. Would you mind looking at them?"

"I suppose so," he answered.

I brought the papers in, and watched as he thumbed through them. "Looks like the real McCoy to me," he finally commented. "Now that you're here, we're going to have a meeting tonight, if you'd care to attend."

"You bet!" I said, trying to calm my excitement of actually finding this place.

"By the way," he added, "you drove in the back way. There is a front way."

Typical! I mused. I could just imagine the beings in their craft somewhere having a good laugh over this one. I was beginning to appreciate their sense of humor, especially at my perceived lack of confidence in their continuing guidance.

The Meeting

That night, people came from all over the United States; some had even flown in for the meeting. The underground room, which was carved out of the rock, was packed. I sat quietly waiting for the meeting to begin. Before long, everyone started to sing... *I'm forever blowing bubbles...*

Good God! I thought. *How absolutely bizarre! Don't tell me this is some kind of cult!* I considered leaving, but my innate sense of curiosity took over, overruling my growing anxiety. I sat still, wondering what would happen next. In a moment, the whole group stopped singing. Then as with one voice, they all began chanting *Ommmmm.* Now I was really blown away!

Mrs. Van Tassel must have sensed my nervousness. She leaned toward me. "We're chanting to raise the vibrations," she whispered.

I studied her closely. *OK...when in Rome....*

Soon George Van Tassel began to speak. But then something even stranger happened. Momentarily, his voice changed...became deeper, a monotone. Whoever was speaking through him now introduced himself as some *space being!* "*... and we are coming from the realms of Blaau...*"

What was going on? What were all these odd sounding names? I had never heard such strange words before. But as I listened, I felt a stirring within—a knowingness that what *he* was saying made sense. *He* was talking about *their* civilization and why *they* were here. It was like a briefing, alerting us to situations that were taking place on the earth and what we humans had to do in order to bring about a peaceful solution to these events. The entity stated that *they* were very upset about atomic devices we were using, and informed us of tactics we could use to change our situation, such as contacting our Congressmen and working as a group.

5

Before the communication ended and Van Tassel came out of his altered state, the entity informed us that their ships would be flying over us in a few minutes. He was right! We all went upstairs and watched as the ships passed in formation overhead. I was in awe.

After the first session, we feasted on coffee and donuts. It was just before the second session was to begin that Mrs. Van Tassel spoke up. "Would Robert Short care to come down and sit with us? I think something interesting might happen here." Her request took me completely by surprise, but nonetheless I complied.

The singing and chanting started again, and as before, Van Tassel went into an altered state. To my utter astonishment, *my* right arm suddenly began to vibrate. Within moments, my entire body was vibrating. *Stop this!* I silently chastised whatever unseen force was causing me to shake. But the vibration did not stop; it only intensified. The next thing I knew...I was out like a light!

It wasn't until sometime later when I came to that I realized people were staring at me. I turned to Van Tassel. "Sorry... I must have fallen asleep," I told him sheepishly.

"Fell asleep, my fanny! Holy Mackerel! How do *they* push a booming sound like that through a set of vocal cords?" Van Tassel stared at me with an amazed look on his face.

I was confused. What was he talking about? And why were all these people staring at me?

"A thundering voice came out of you," Van Tassel continued. "It exploded and rang off the rocks in the room!"

"But I thought I just fell asleep. I don't remember anything."

"Sleep, you didn't! No Sir...that voice..."

"What did the voice say?" I interrupted him. I was still confused as to what had just transpired.

"The being who spoke through you said that *they* wished the people peace, blessings and love, and were most happy that these people were here to receive this information. Then *he* stopped speaking and signed off."

6

"But who was *he*?" I wanted to know. "What was *his* name?"

"It sounded like Juneau…or Junal…something like that," Van Tassel informed me.

"Could it have been Jon-al?" I questioned.

"Yeah, that could have been it," Van Tassel said.

I was close to tears. I had discovered that I could really do it—*I could actually go into an altered state!* I went back to Giant Rock every month, going through the same experiences. It was like being in training. I also continued with the automatic writing, eventually forming a group in North Hollywood where we continued our ongoing communication with the *Extraterrestrial Intelligence*.

CHAPTER TWO
CONTACT

On Highway 62, between Yucca Valley and Joshua Tree, California, sits a town called Paradise Valley. In 1958, there were few houses around. It was the 10th of October and I was staying with a friend. Just after 8:00 p.m., with some fading daylight still in the sky, I decided to take an evening walk down the road.

Suddenly, my eyes focused on a saucer-shaped object hovering just above the ground and about one and a half football fields away. It looked to be approximately 35 feet in diameter and about 20 feet tall, with a domed top. As I stood looking at the object, an intense bluish-white light shot from the craft's underside. The light startled me, forcing me to look away momentarily. When I was again able to focus on the craft, I was amazed to discover that a hatch had mysteriously opened in its side. The heat of the day had subsided, but profuse beads of sweat now trickled down my face and neck, dampening my clothes. A lump of apprehension lodged in my throat. Although over the years I had accepted *mental* contact with the beings, this spontaneous and fear provoking reaction to a *physical* close encounter was overwhelming and not something that I had anticipated. I only knew that whatever this object was, it was headed for me! My first instinct was to run. But as if paralyzed, my legs wouldn't move. I stood frozen in my tracks, hardly able to breathe. I could do nothing but watch.

The being that came out of the ship was human looking, about 5'10" with a well-chiseled face, high cheekbones and shoulder-length hair that blew slightly in the breeze. It was astounding. As humanoid as this being appeared, I knew without a doubt that I was about to come face-to-face with someone from *another world*. Fragmented thoughts tumbled through my mind, as my so-called "normal" reality became disjointed, quickly crumbling before my mind's eye. Would I even be able to stand up, or were my knees about to buckle? Then, while in the midst of all this strangeness, I did something totally unexpected. As the being approached within arm's reach, I put out my hand in greeting. To reciprocate, the being placed his hand over his heart as if to say, *Everything that I am, everything that you see, is open to you.*

Immediately, my mind cleared. The panic I had experienced upon first seeing the craft and the being who disembarked from it was now gone. I had never felt this alive…ever. I was infused with a tremendous sense of peace and well being. The humanoid seemed to be able to look right through me. Instinctively, I knew that he had knowledge of everything about me from even before my birth, and up to the present.

We had to come down to make an adjustment in the power of our craft, the being informed me. *We will see you at a future time.*

How could he say those words and yet his lips never moved? I wondered. (I later learned that even while appearing in the physical, all communication with these particular beings is telepathic). With that, the being turned and walked back to the spacecraft. *Please don't leave me here!* I telepathically called to him. It seemed odd at the time that I would even make such a request. In a moment, the craft appeared to rise about 100 feet into the air, then suddenly disappear into the night sky. For the longest time, I stood looking into the vastness of space, wondering when that *"future time"* when *"we would see each other again"* would come.

I have never forgotten this first physical encounter with a being who later described himself as a member of a *Solar Confederation.* But no matter how many accounts of physical contact I heard or read about over the years, I still felt somewhat alone in my experience. No one had yet described specifics of their own encounters with extraterrestrials that directly correlated with my own; that is until I met Landi Mellas, who agreed to help with the editing of this book. Through her, I came to know David Caywood.

Landi and David had just co-authored their own book, *The Other Sky*, published October, 2002. As Landi shared with me David's experience, and David later discussed the experience in detail, I could not hold back my emotions. Tears flooded my eyes; tears that told me that I was not alone. Someone else understood. David related that he also had felt very alone. Until now, no one had described with such similarity his own encounter. This connection between David, Landi, and myself, is just one more synchronicity that awakens me to the understanding that we are but a very small part of the universal whole.

A Traducere Lumina–Translator of Light

Where does the information that I receive as a "channel" come from, and by what methods does it get here? In our terms, the methods are called *Translators* or *Tensors*. The *beings* term it *Instruct Relay* (Automatic Translator).

Chronomonitor describes a *time-period* or *scanning of time* through the Subspace Radio Network in our system down through a number of planetary craft (UFOs) in our space corridors and atmospheric levels to the *monitoring devices* (scanners). From here, the information is sent to the *Instruments* or *Translators*. These *Instruments* and *Translators* include human channelers, television devices, radio communication, vast distance communication, called *radar telephonic*, and lastly, through the mind's ability to send images over distances, called *telepathy*. There are many different modes, but these, in brief, are the methods. The engineering technology of some of these may be beyond our present comprehension.

The *Instrument* (or Channeler, as I am called) receives a highly accelerated *code form* through the brain area called the bridge or pons. This bridge links the two occiputs of the brain, located near the diencephalon (hind brain or nub ending) of the sympathetic trunk nerve. This then acts to *translate* the code and affects the *inner auditory* (inner ear) along with the pineal cortex, which in turn creates

10

imagery that one can comprehend. The occiputs and cells of the cranial area scan these images and translate them into our known equivalence in whatever language and nation the information is directed. Thus, when the *Instrument* (channeler) speaks, they are known as the *Translator*. In terms of the greater understanding of the S*pace Intelligence*, this is referred to as a TRADUCERE LUMINA (defined as one who bridges the gap; one who crosses over; one who goes before - a Translator), or a TRANSLATOR OF LIGHT!

The Reality of UFOs

I will begin from the premise that many are now prepared to accept the fact that these aerial objects do exist, even if they have not as yet been fortunate enough to see them.

British Air Chief Marshall Lord Dowding once commented: "Of course, the Flying Saucers are real ... and they are interplanetary."

As the author, I can speak with conviction and some authority on extraterrestrial craft, because I have been privileged to watch them. I have also studied the phenomena for over fifty years and personally know other reliable witnesses who would have preferred *not* to have seen them. Apart from personal convictions, there exists accumulative evidence of genuine sightings and landings world-wide since World War II. At that time, they were seen over all the theaters of war (see the observations of "foo fighters"). Prior to that time, strange visitation to this planet is recorded in history.

According to Major Donald Keyhoe, formerly of the United States Marines, who wrote four rational books on this subject and had access to some of the United States Defense Department files, at the time of his writings, there had been 25,000 confirmed sightings in the USA since 1946. That was a *conservative estimate*, and doubtless, according to estimates, there had been 250 or more UFO crashes.

You will appreciate that this is a vast subject, and I can do little more than give an outline of some of the facts. As yet, none is a full answer as to why *they* are here. However, I do hope to stimulate your interest and awaken your imagination, for indeed, "there are more things in Heaven and Earth than are dreamed of in your philosophy."

It is not possible for me to give an appraisal from the scientific or technical approach. But as a philosopher, I would offer food for thought. We are living in a period of great change in which we shall find ourselves moving away from the entrenched materialism of the past century and into new realms of thought and greater understanding. If we are to survive the hazards of the times just ahead, then we must find a more balanced and intelligent approach to life in the cosmos, and the infinite intelligence behind all these creations.

Unidentified Flying Objects—What Are They?

Unidentified Flying Objects are just that—objects seen in our skies that cannot be identified by our present knowledge of man-made technology. For those who have seen and studied these objects, it is thought that they might be *space vehicles* that are automatically or intelligently controlled. That a few may be controlled by *pre-programmed intelligence* has also been considered. There are several forms of UFOs most frequently seen:

The Discs—often described as *flying saucers* because they are shaped like inverted saucers or soup plates and travel in the environs of this planet. They are generally 25 to 30 feet in diameter, but do vary; some larger, some smaller, such as small spheroids. When close enough to be observed in any detail, the discs have a domed top which sometimes displays windows or portholes.

The Cigar-shape—a larger craft estimated to be miles in length (according to trained observers). These are thought to be *Inter-stellar or Outer-Space (Intergalactic) craft-carriers,* since the smaller disc-like objects have on occasion been seen either entering or leaving these larger ships when stationed high in our atmosphere. The cigar-shaped craft have shown openings through which the discs move, and some are seen with windows along their sides. However, these larger craft do not necessarily carry smaller craft.

Luminous Ephemeral Spheres of Light—These spheres of light are semi-transparent in appearance and radiate powerful colors, often a deep orange glow. Some refer to these as *Monitors* or *Scanners*. Seen in normal daylight and good weather conditions, the discs and craft-carriers are a metallic gray or silver. However, these ephemeral objects are frequently seen as brilliant white lights in the sky, so dazzling that the actual form behind the light is masked and cannot be scrutinized visually, even with other aids.

Their Revolutionary Construction

There would appear to be a measure of ionization in the construction of these spacecraft as their color changes with any alteration in speed. Thus a white object in motion might seem to change color from white to cream, yellow, green, orange, or red, often before vanishing from sight. I have personally witnessed this, and I am given to understand that when ionized, different gases yield different colors.

The fantastic speeds at which these craft move, their silent vertical ascent and descent, and their incredible maneuvers and equally silent transits place them and their construction beyond our conventional aircraft.[1] Some exhibit a "pendulum" movement by swinging from side-to-side like a falling leaf, or they remain motionless and silent in mid-air. They make right-angled turns, and when they spin on their axis, they often exhibit glittering red, green, white and blue lights. While in the presence of these craft, some people have been conscious of a humming sound like bees in a hive, or a slight swishing sound as they move vertically. There have also been reports of every other imaginable sound, depending on a number of factors.

---

[1] 1 May 1952 "PROJECT MAGNET" – CANADA reported a disc's speed at 3,600 mph.

Information relayed through my own contact with *Space Intelligence* gives us further insight into the construction of these craft. They explain that the moldings for their spaceships are manufactured in one piece, having an atomic number and matrix that is so tightly intersticed that it is impossible for it to be destroyed, unless under a pressure of a force greater than that which operates these types of craft. They are formed by certain methods which as yet are unknown to ordinary design. Illumination onboard their craft is electroluminescent and is created by a secondary motive force. This interactive force creates a coronal discharge which gives off various colors of angstrom rating of electromagnetic spectrum as the craft goes through differential speed ratios. Energy fields onboard are always maintained; the used energy replaced or restored through a differential accumulator which keeps a numbered record of energy particles, releasing or returning such energy particles as needed to maintain a balance of energy. This allows for the maintenance of artificial atmospheric conditions within the various sectors of the interior of the craft which coincide with atmospheric conditions upon the surface of various planets.

I am also informed that these craft are equipped with certain weaponry for protection or defense, but this weaponry is only used when under attack by other more negative forces, such as those who have committed unacceptable experimentation with our own populace.

It would also seem that the *Space Intelligence* has a more enlightened understanding of death and regeneration of physical matter than we have at present, for if they should meet with transition or death by war or some other means, they have the decision of returning to embodiment by a certain scientific process of which *they* have knowledge.

My *source* further states that several levels of our military-industrial complex have some information of the construction of these craft, but it is limited. There is much beyond this limited knowledge which is presently used by intelligence on other worlds, but is still an unknown factor on this planet. Perhaps in the future, this knowledge will become more known and will be used in traveling to our moon and other planets in our solar system. Our knowledge of spaceship design for traveling into deep space and beyond is also limited at present.

According to the *Space Intelligence*, one of the early "contactees," George Adamski, whom we will discuss in a later chapter, was known to them. Adamski referred to these spaceships and those who ride in them as "friends from another planetary system" who spoke to him and described these spaceships as "Crystal Bells." This descriptive name was given because of the craft's stabilizer and other operating equipment sounding very much like bells when struck. Adamski also stated, "As I looked up at the shuttle craft I could see two other individuals as though through a transparency in the side of the craft." These older types of spaceships, according to the *Space Intelligence*, are still used to travel down and back again to their carriers and *seem* to appear transparent. While in movement, the stabilizer ring about the perimeter of the craft's circumference creates a sound much like glass that is manufactured from crystal. When struck, this sounds like a bell. Some of these craft have stabilizers that are counter-rotating, so as to form differential balance levels with one another while maintaining hovering position. (This could be similar to the use of the oscillating gimbal devices on our rockets allowing for attitude correction while orbiting the planet, or for correcting directional thrust while moving toward and into orbital speed). These stabilizers at times emit a very high frequency sound which may rise above our decibel range. Perhaps this is why so many witnesses to UFOs describe the hovering craft as "silent."

Since that time period when George Adamski's experience took place, there have been many individuals who have been witness to other types of spaceship design.However, these other types still retain the basics of what has been stated. Many of these craft may be from civilizations and planetary systems other than that of my *source*; nonetheless, the name "Crystal Bell" seems to apply in most cases.

What Are Their Sources of Origin?

Just exactly where UFOs come from is a question that has taxed the minds of the experts and public alike. Originally the military thought that they originated from other countries such as Germany, Russia or China, but this was discounted long ago. It is now thought by some that these craft may come from *inside the earth* via the polar openings, which may be entrances to other dimensions.[2] There is also a theory that the earth is hollow. It is my belief that the earth is not really hollow, although it may have many large caverns and tunnels. Archeologists have found some evidence of this in different parts of the world. There is also some talk of late of a "Secret UFO City" somewhere in South America. Other hypotheses propose that these craft might come from other planets in our own solar system, or from other systems or galaxies—even from interdimensional realms. With regard to the interdimensional hypothesis, some of the craft have been known to change shape and substance, moving from an apparently solid body to a semi-transparent state before vanishing from visual sight. Such craft have been labeled "mutants" by one physicist, and are difficult to explain.

The accumulated evidence for vehicles changing in form and substance, materializing in empty space, or dematerializing in a flash, suggests that they and their occupants are able to come into our third dimensional world from other dimensional levels, where intelligent beings exist in frequencies which render their presence invisible to us. This concept is steadily gaining ground as the materialism of

---

[2] A photo of the North Pole opening was taken by an American satellite on 23 November 1968 and shows a presumed or claimed hole in the center of the earth. This picture was published by Raymond Palmer in his "Flying Saucer" magazine.

science over the past century yields to a more enlightened and comprehensive understanding of both mind and matter. In 1926, Rutherford and Bohr, in their brilliant analysis of the atom, discovered a unit of energy. The electrons of the atom were found to be moving around the nucleus in a similar manner to the planets in our system orbiting the sun. There is now a growing awareness that our world of the third dimension, which is limited by our five senses, is *not* the extent of creation!

There are, of course, dense physical third-dimensional worlds contained within the confines of the infra-red and ultra-violet spectrum, but they would now appear to be one tiny aspect of planetary and solar creations. Beyond those limitations are thought to exist other unseen worlds peopled by intelligent life and clad in bodies appropriate to their planetary or solar conditions. They are existing in dimensions of which we are not presently aware, because they live within a faster vibrational frequency rate which renders them invisible to our normal sight. Such a hypothesis would account for incidents which are otherwise extremely difficult to fathom. For example: An *alien craft* is seen visually and appears on a radar screen. A jet is "scrambled" to intercept the unknown. The pilot appears to be on a collision course with the craft when it vanishes from his sight, yet still shows up as a silver "blip" on the radarscope! As explained to me by my *Extraterrestrial Source*, some of these visitors are able to render themselves and their craft invisible to normal sight by what *they* refer to as "powering up." We might refer to it as "stealth."

The hypothesis postulates realms of creation which are beyond us and with which, I suspect, we are to become acquainted in the years ahead. Most of us are not ready for this yet. However, we are moving in the right direction when we accept that appearances are deceptive; that matter is no longer solid but made up of units of energy; and that mind is capable of manipulating matter in ways we do not understand—yet. Therefore, the answer to the question: "Where do *they* come from?" is not an easy one to deal with.

Since many of these spacecraft appear to be solid enough to leave evidence of their presence on our soil and crops, they could come from other third-dimensional planets within and beyond our solar system, and cultures far in advance of us in every way. It is suggested that many of these extraterrestrials are morally and spiritually superior because they seem to have advanced to their present level of evolution without destroying themselves. We should not dismiss as nonsense the interdimensional hypothesis, and should bear in mind that there is already talk of parallel universes and anti-matter mentioned in science fiction, and now spoken of as fact.

The massive *craft-carriers* would seem to be from outer space, whereas the smaller *disc-shaped craft* are released into our atmosphere. This suggests that these smaller discs have a limited range of travel and facilities, and are literally "scout ships" cruising within the environs of a planet, unable to travel long distances outside our atmosphere except for those with possible "hyper-drive."

The following was received through my contact with *Space Intelligence* as clarification of these craft and their origin. *They* refer to "Mother Ships" as "Klactas." The *Space Intelligence* states:

> These "Klactas" can be enormous, and can be compared to a traveling planetoid body that hypothetically carries a population as large as many thousands of inhabitants without ever coming into contact with another planet. We, Space Intelligence, had stated to the one known as George Adamski, that in an emergency, our shuttle craft could remove the entire population of New York City and still have room left on our largest carriers. In a linear sense, some of these craft may be many miles long with a circumference of many tens of miles. These Klactas, or Mother Ships, maintain themselves entirely as a self-

18

contained traveling city, and may contain as many as 50 of the smaller shuttle-type craft. These shuttle craft are approximately 36 feet in circumference and 20 feet from the magnetic grid plate (bottom center of craft) to the top cupola or dome, and might carry as many as 100 or as few as 20 crew members, depending upon their size and purpose. In turn, these shuttle craft may release even smaller "monitors" or "scanners." There are some upon your planet earth that have been aboard certain of these craft, but have been shown through only a small section of the craft called "Klacteem." These Klacteem sections are approximately 168 feet long with a circumference of approximately 70 feet.

The fact that these huge Klactas can exist in space may be somewhat startling to your thought processes; nonetheless, once you understand and overcome the resistance of centrifugal and centripetal forces reacting against an aircraft's airfoils design and constructed materials, then it would become possible to move by maintaining amplified gravitational fields and coordinates of differential speed ratio. This can be used to travel into spatial parsecs and vectors, such as your type of rocketry carries out in moving into a given orbit. However, unless the orbit is maintained by the continuous use of its given differential speed ratio, the orbit could decay and fall back by the push-pull of earth's gravitational influence. Our Space Intelligence ships are able to enter into energy states that are inframural in dimension, thus projecting through what is called the "time barrier" or "light fields." Our own physical

19

bodies go through this same dimensional shift; that is, there is a substantial point in terms of differential speed ratio where the molecular energy may be projected from one dimension to another. The demolecularization then takes place with the spaceship and its occupants remaining physically intact. This projection is done by numerical sequence so that we are at all times aware of the time elements and that which takes place in differential energy fields in terms of their speed ratio in nanoseconds (atomic time). The interchange of energy in terms of particles takes on an appearance of "time standing still" as we pass from one differential time field to another. There is, however, the possibility of magnetic confluence disturbance (magnetic storms) that can place those who travel the corridors of space in a rather precarious situation. It is during these disturbances that we do not travel interdimensionally, but wait until the "storm" lifts, when passage through what has been called the "Seven Rings Pass Not" is resumed.

CHAPTER THREE
HERE, THERE, AND EVERYWHERE

Is There a Behavior Pattern Forming?

UFOs have been seen all over the world in increasing numbers since World War II. They have been reported world-wide by Army, Navy and Air Force personnel. They are seen by scientists, astronomers, engineers, ground staff at air bases; doctors, police, and schoolmasters, as well as ordinary citizens—even children in school. Airline pilots and crews have also witnessed them.

In 1947, Kenneth Arnold, an American businessman who was flying his own aircraft, reported seeing nine discs flying over Mount Rainier, Washington. They were, he estimated, one hundred feet in diameter, and they flew in perfect coordination of movement. He was quick to observe that those in cloud-shadow were a metallic gray in color, while the others shone like gold in the sunlight.

According to available records, the number of sightings has steadily increased in Britain and overseas. In recent years, there has also been an increase in the number of landings and near-landings, as well as claimed "personal contacts" with space crew members.

In July 1954, an Australian UFO Research Group stated: "We are fully agreed that these things are material objects and not optical illusions or hallucinations. They are getting lower, seemingly to land."

Many of these landings have left marks on the ground or other physical indications. Take for example incidents near the sugar plantations at Tully, 1,150 miles north of Brisbane in Queensland, Australia. The farmers have spotted landed vehicles, and after their departure have examined the area to find that the reeds were flattened in a circular pattern resulting from the actual landing or vertical take-off from the ground. Samples of earth and reeds were sent to Queensland University for tests.

21

Humanoid or robotic appearing forms that have emerged from grounded vehicles have been observed taking water from our lakes and rivers. They have also been observed taking samples of plants, crops, soil and rocks, or merely adjusting or repairing equipment connected with the craft. According to my *source*, the water taken from our planet is for coolant purposes for their craft, and then only in an emergency. Some who have been witness to this "taking up" of water from our lakes and rivers perceive a form of ionization surrounding the craft which is similar to a cloud. I am told that this is often done to make it easier for the *beings* to observe our planet without themselves being observed. In some cases, this ionization will totally conceal the spacecraft, but when photographs of these unusual "clouds" are taken, they reveal the presence of spaceships!

You will appreciate that these are proofs of objectivity, which is probably the main reason for the landings and occasionally letting themselves be seen— perhaps a program of "getting to know you." Or the extraterrestrials may, of course, be interested in the general state of pollution on earth!

Near-landings on or near main roads and motorways throughout America, Canada, France and England, and elsewhere in remote or sparsely populated areas, have caused car lights to dim and engines to cut out. This renders the vehicles inoperable until the craft, which has landed or is hovering near the vehicle, decides to depart from the scene. Afterwards, the lights and engine power have been fully re-stored without any damage to the vehicles or the occupants.[3] There are technical explanations for the malfunctioning of electrical circuits and magnetic devices which stem from the belief that the force fields or method of propulsion of these craft are electromagnetic. Ley lines, or rods of power, including large KV power lines run like a grid around the earth's surface and are thought to be drawn on for magnetic

---

[3] Some cars and their occupants have been lifted, carried several miles, and then replaced on the ground.

energy. This, however, is a field of study for expert engineers interested in this subject.

The number of such "close encounters" of this nature is steadily increasing. Person-to-person contacts have occurred in Europe, South America, the United States, Scandinavia, and Canada, and without a doubt every other country in the world. There have also been alleged abduction cases where human beings have been taken into spacecraft and later released. These cannot be ignored on the evidence secured. Moreover, there is a presumption that selected engineers in the United States and probably in other technically advanced countries in the West have been *invited* to inspect the inside of some of the landed craft. To my knowledge, there are two recorded instances to which the engineers in question have spoken or published papers on their experiences.[4]

Craft Controlled by Intelligence

It will be realized from the foregoing details that there is some form of *intelligent life* manning many of these craft, and that these *beings* are scientifically and technologically ahead of us. It is also felt that although some UFOs are no doubt automatically controlled, still others may be projected images or holograms.

Among these *visitors* there would appear to be at least two groups engaged in this exploration of our planet— the one positive, friendly, and courteous; the other, unfriendly, sometimes malicious, and at times known to harm or confuse people. Fortunately, from the statistics and known facts, the latter group is the minority. It is a reality

---

[4] George Van Tassel in California, USA. Also, Dr. Daniel Fry in New Mexico, during his period of service at White Sands Proving Grounds, was invited aboard a remotely controlled craft from space and was in constant telepathic communication with a being who said he might be identified as *Alan.*

that some persons have certainly experienced negative interaction with extraterrestrial beings; their frightening stories of abductions and medical examinations aboard alien craft cause fear in our hearts. Even in the world of extraterrestrials, there appears to be a duality—those who would take advantage of the human race, and those who are truly concerned for the welfare of our planet and for humanity. Unfortunately, as is often the case on planet earth, our lower emotions seem to call out loudly for attention; thus the negative sometimes receives more notoriety than the positive.

What Do "Space People" Look Like?

Many of the beings who are interacting with us are similar to ourselves in appearance, but details do vary. This is to be expected when we think about people on our own planet who display differences in features, pigment, hair color, height and build, to say nothing of the effect of variations in climate and geophysical conditions on their general appearance, taste, conduct, culture and beliefs. Therefore, it is reasonable to conclude that life on other third-dimensional planets in this or other systems will be varied, as will logic and time.

Some of these *visitors* are noted to be very tall and slender, fair of hair and skin, and of noble appearance. On the other hand, there are seen *little people* not more than three and a half to five feet in height, rather like our Kalahari Desert pygmies in Africa. These humanoid types seem to predominate among the *visitors,* if we can accept the reports of "contactees" throughout the world. Beings similar to ourselves have been encountered in countries such as France, the United States, Brazil, Peru, Russia, South Africa, Australia and Britain, to name just a few. Other varied but less common descriptions of beings have also been reported. There have even been reports of strange creatures with an unpleasant odor, wearing cumbersome garments, and helmeted beings in heavy space garb who move about like our own astronauts, being unaccustomed to our gravity.

Is Intelligent Communication With These Visitors Possible?

Up to a point, intelligent communication with some of these visitors has been possible. Casual interchanges would not seem of much value except to possibly establish a friendly link, and again that may be the point in many cases. *Go and show yourselves to the people,* seems to be a phrase often ringing in my own ears these days. It is the general consensus that the majority of those people who are considered "abductees" have reported *some* communication with their abductors; however, this communication has many times seemed to be one-sided; the abductors giving the orders; the abductee following the orders. But again there are other reports of humans carrying on intelligent and detailed exchange with the visitors.

Radio, radio-telegraphy, electronic beams and telepathy have been used in the past, and are still currently being used and maintained among selected "contacts" throughout the western world. From various sources of information collected as evidence, these forms of communication are also being used presumably in C.S.I. (what is now Russia) and in other parts of the world.

It is important that the telepathic link should also be recognized, or the possibility of telepathy accepted, because we are in the process of moving into a new evolutionary phase in which such faculties will be developed in mankind. After all, we are not in fact using the whole of our brain. Telepathy has actually been researched since the early part of the 20th century.

What Does The Public Think?

Only to a degree is it possible to access what the public thinks regarding UFOs and alien contact. To my knowledge, surveys have been undertaken in Great Britain, Belgium and the United States, where so much seems to be happening all the time. A large percentage of people are beginning to give the matter serious thought, some surmising the objects as secret weapons launched by the military. [5] The plain fact that these aeroforms are seen all over the world seems to make no difference to this approach.

There are some groups who are interested in the scientific aspect of the phenomena, accepting them as spacecraft from a more advanced civilization. These groups are interested in the means of propulsion, speed, maneuvers, structure, size and gravity clearance. There are other groups, however, who are mainly interested in where *they* come from and why *they* are here in our skies in increasing numbers. It is now estimated from *updated* investigated UFO reports that there have been over 250 million known sightings worldwide since 1947, and over 250,000 contacts.

The United States experienced mass sightings in different parts of the continent in the 1940's, mid 1950's and mid 1960's. South Africa, Australia, New Zealand and Mexico have experienced much activity in recent years. In 1952 there occurred the "July Flap" when UFOs were over the White House in our own capital city of Washington, D.C. for two hours! A pattern of gradual acceptance is now seen emerging around the world, with more and more people ready to accept these objects as interplanetary machines, intelligently controlled by beings who in the main wish us no harm. Fifty-four percent or more of the American people now believe this, and also that the craft are manned by beings not unlike us in many ways; hence, the present preoccupation with space, science-fiction books and movies.

The Continuing Conspiracy of Silence

No talk on this subject would be complete without special reference to the willful conspiracy of silence on the part of the authorities throughout the world. The establishments of the most powerful nations on earth show

---

[5] See Nevada test site, Groom Lake and S-4, as well as that called the "Ant Hill" in the Tehachapi Mountains of Southern California, USA.

little sign of breaking down under public pressure. Yet it is known that the Defense Departments of the major powers have access to files of evidence compiled over the past fifty-five years and have sworn all personnel, including civilian airline pilots involved in those sightings and records, to secrecy, with dire punishments for those who dare to disobey.

There are governments in the world who have publicly given recognition to the phenomena as intelligently controlled extraterrestrial spacecraft. Norway, Belgium, South Africa, Australia, Peru, Brazil, Argentina, Venezuela and Canada are but a few. This means that the "Great Powers" are either unprepared, or unwilling, to reveal their information and conclusions to the multitudes in the world who continue to remain in ignorance.

In his book *UFO's: The Psychic Solution*, the eminent French physicist, Jacques Vallee, discusses three types of cover-up:

First, individuals reporting sightings are pressured to be silent about them, and authorities who receive reports from Defense (AFR 200-2) or other personnel, including scientists, law enforcement, pilots (JANAP 142) and astronomers, are cautioned to remain silent under instructions from some higher nameless power or authority.

The American Air Force has been seen to take some action on account of widespread public pressure when PROJECT SIGN was set up in 1947 to investigate—and then conceal the truth from the public. In 1950, PROJECT SIGN was changed to PROJECT GRUDGE when saucer reports swamped the United States Air Force. In 1952, PROJECT GRUDGE was changed to PROJECT BLUE BOOK, which was set up under Captain Edward Ruppelt of the United States Air Force. This project existed until 1966 when it was presumed closed down. However, reported waves of sightings across the states forced the defense authorities to set up a so-called "independent" non-military body to continue to investigate the phenomena in 1967 under the leadership of Dr. Edward Condon. This was known as the

CONDON PROJECT. Out of this came the famous, or infamous, CONDON REPORT, the findings of which were widely known to be "rigged." When this was discovered by Dr. Frank Salisbury, who was part of the investigation team, he immediately resigned. Those involved in the Condon Report were instructed at the outset to make a negative report, and all "sound" evidence handed over to them from the American Air Force files and records from other sources were then destroyed. The best evidence was never given to them. Their findings were based on a small percentage of selected cases, and *not* on free access to the *thousands* of filed reports from trained observers and others being held as "Classified" or "Top Secret - Eyes Only" material. As a consequence, independent research groups were created in the United States and in other parts of the world. To this day, many scientists, engineers and other specialists work in secret because of the official attitude to clamp down! They do not want their own findings to be confiscated. This has also been shown in the explorations of the NASA programs and their astronauts and personnel.

The second cover-up involved the official release of various explanations prepared to discredit witnesses who spoke out. Their evidence was ridiculed or explained away by ludicrous notions which the long-suffering American people soon learned to mistrust and dismiss. Such incidents have happened in this country, and doubtless in other countries.

Members of the Armed Forces (especially Air Force personnel), police, airline pilots and crews, and other trained observers, have been cross-examined and then allegedly ridiculed by their support officers. This has had the effect, intentional or otherwise, of stopping personnel from reporting sightings.

Members of the public have also reported sightings which have been ignored for the most part. If the case has been substantiated with photographs or other witnesses, then many questions have been asked. Evidence has been confiscated when it has taken the form of either photographs

28

of aeroforms, marks on the ground where craft have landed, or debris thought to be connected with such craft.[6] Often witnesses are asked to remain silent about their experience, and many independent investigators have been silenced through methods of intimidation by mysterious men whose main aim has been to see that lips are sealed. Their tactics are similar to those of the Mafia or CIA.[7]

According to Major Donald Keyhoe, who has commented in his book *Aliens From Space* as to the effects of the phenomena on the authorities and personnel, the Armed Services personnel are sworn not to reveal any details or facts to anyone. Any serviceman found guilty of this offense will be heavily fined, or serve a term of imprisonment as long as ten years, or both. Some of the most intelligent writers and researchers into the phenomena have commented on the fact that some people who knew too much and expressed the will to speak out so that mankind might know the truth were found dead in suspicious circumstances.

The third cover-up to which Jacques Vallee has referred is based on his own knowledge and contact with well-informed sources of information. Many ordinary people are afraid to speak out and describe what they have seen or experienced for a number of personal reasons—although fear of ridicule by the press, their neighbors, or co-workers may play a part in this reluctance. These people may be fearful of being regarded as mentally unbalanced.

Nevertheless, it is well known that people seem to react in one of two ways to the phenomena. Either they feel serene and spiritually uplifted by the experience, or apprehensive and fearful. Where there has been personal contact or close encounter, the information given them is many times fragmentary and often confusing. This is understandable in light of the great differences which must

---

[6] See Philip J. Corso's book *The Day After Roswell*
[7] See discussion regarding a mysterious group called: "MJ-12, or Majestic Twelve."

exist between ourselves and *beings* coming from more advanced evolutionary levels of existence. There would seem to be many levels of contact, and many levels of knowledge and understanding. Some of the people who have these unexpected contact experiences might not necessarily be well-educated or well-informed. Some may be entirely ignorant of the concept of intelligent life in the universe. Indeed, it is often to the poor and humble people that an approach is made. Hopefully, this cover-up of the knowledge and reality of extraterrestrial spacecraft by our major world governments will one day come to an end. All of us who have had personal experience with UFOs and their occupants can only hope that day will be soon.

CHAPTER FOUR
LOOKING FOR ANSWERS

Why Are *They* Here?

Sometimes, when faced with a difficult problem to resolve, we can arrive at a solution only if we approach it from a position of higher awareness.

A minority of investigators have come up with an answer which might surprise us, and which we may find totally unacceptable according to where we stand in our own personal development. However, I ask that you give serious consideration to the following, because it does offer many pieces which would actually fit into this great cosmic jigsaw puzzle—if we would only take the time and the extra effort to carefully examine them.

I will present you with a few leads. To arrive at these leads to a possible solution as to why *they* are here, it has been necessary to research outside the main theme of this book.

Cosmology – The Neglected Science

Cosmology, a combination of astronomy and astrology, was regarded by the ancient priesthoods of Egypt and other civilizations as a sacred science. Fragments which have survived in Western culture tell us that our solar system moves through one constellation in the twelve signs of the Zodiac in approximately 2,150 years, termed an *Age* or *Cycle*. This period of time varies somewhat. For our solar system to move in the direction of all twelve signs or constellations in the Zodiac, it takes an estimated period of 25,800 to 26,000 years.

It is highly probable that we have now arrived at the final *Age of the Zodiacal Time-Cycle,* which happened to coincide with the termination not only of the *Piscean Age,* but also with the culmination of greater *Cosmic Time Cycles.* This could mean that something of great significance is about to happen in the very near future—probably in our lifetime.

Cosmology indicates that external influences from other planetary and star bodies influence the planets and sun in our own system, and that there are periodic celestial and terrestrial upheavals toward the end of each *Age* or *Cycle*. These upheavals happen as the solar system moves from one *Cycle* to the next. We are now experiencing geophysical and other environmental upheavals on the planet, partly because we are in the actual interim period between the last *Age* and the present so-called *Aquarian Age*. We have yet to see the further development of the planet Jupiter, possibly as a sun (to create a binary system of two suns) and the results of the *Planetary Alignment of 1982*, as well as the *Grand Alignment of 1962*. We now have it reported that there is apparently the appearance of Zecharia Sitchin's planetary body named "Nebiru!"[8]

History is cyclical, *not* linear! It has all happened before in the sense that the Greeks and their contemporaries of other civilizations and cultures referred to the *Age of Aquarius* as the *Age of Saturn* or *Golden Age* in which the Gods come to earth, and a new and beautiful civilization is born!

In accordance with cosmic laws controlling the evolution of men, planets and suns, mutational changes take place from time-to-time to assist in the spiritual development of men as Sons of God.[9] Such a change is due now, and it will affect the atomic structure of the earth and its inhabitants. This is a big subject in itself to which I could not give enough time now. We find difficulty understanding how these *Cyclic Changes* come into being, i.e. the mechanics of change, but quite obviously there are metaphysical influences at work all the time. Higher powers

---

[8] See Zecharia Sitchin's *The Twelfth Planet*
[9] See "Photon Belt" references in book by Sheldon Nidle, *We Are Becoming Galactic Humans.*

of great magnitude bring into periodical manifestation cosmic laws with which we are not yet acquainted in accordance with the dynamics of the universe.

The Rise and Fall of Civilizations

We come now to the next lead which may have bearing on the question of why UFOs and extraterrestrials are here. The late historian, Arnold Toynbee, was aware of the rapid decline of Western civilization. He observes that all historians have no difficulty in tracing the causes which led to the downfall of a civilization, but were at a loss to account for the rise of the next one. Finally, after deep thought and much research, Toynbee came to the conclusion that the Bible offers clues which might give the answer. I think, by implication, he was saying that help has to come from *outside the planet.*

I will leave you to be the final judge as to whether one should give credence to his following conclusions.

According to ancient sacred traditions, mankind knew other worlds were inhabited by beings who were like men in appearance, only wiser and nobler, whom mankind venerated as "The Gods." These traditions indicate that the gods lived among the stars. The same Eastern and Western traditions of an early period tell us that these gods descend to earth at the end and the beginning of each *Age*, and that they come down to teach man how to live! After a suitable period of time, these gods then withdraw, returning to their own habitats among the stars.

Later traditions still speak of "the sons of God" and the "angels" (messengers of the gods) coming to earth. They also speak of the return of the *Promised One,* the World Teacher and Ruler, who would restore peace and order on earth. All the great religions teach this, and many people accept this teaching and await this event.

Bridging the Gap

Since I see it as my task to build bridges, here is an

attempt to bridge the gap between the ancient traditions and the events of today.

There is a modern school of thought among veteran UFO investigators and scientists which says: "We are property!" This may sound rather ominous, but there just might be some truth in the idea. The roots of the hypothesis are to be found in the ancient legend in the Bible of a war in the heavens between two antagonists who struggle for control of planet earth, including its resources and peoples. Sections of humanity worldwide who accept this peculiar idea as fact are aware of what is now happening and the eventual outcome of the age-old struggle which is to end soon.

Doubtless you will find these leads quite incredible, but I would remind you that so often "truth is stranger than fiction," and that fiction these days is often fact tomorrow!

Finally, a word about the "telepathic factor." During the past 50 years, the *Space Intelligence* have selected and systematically trained telepathic "sensitives" all over the world. Perhaps this was done in order that humanity would no longer live in total ignorance of events to come, but would be prepared to a limited degree for fundamental changes to take effect at the end of this 26,000 year cycle. This time was known to the ancient priesthoods as a *Tiger Sun-Cycle*. Among the information given to us by the *Space Intelligence,* we find the following, some of which has already happened.

First; confirmation that the earth is now radioactive and heavily polluted, including our water cycle. Secondly; that we are moving from the third dimension to the fourth-dimensional frequency. This means we shall experience a different time-scale. And thirdly; the whole atomic structure of this planet and humanity will be changed. The moment of infinite change will be sudden, as in the "twinkling of an eye," occurring when the already changing vibrational frequencies are at the right pitch for this to take place. This change will bring about earth changes worldwide.

These situations are thought to be unchangeable in

accordance with the dynamics of the cosmos; that is, we cannot stop them. However, the negative influences presently at work in the world *can* be stopped and are to be removed from the planet shortly. These negative influences are instigating world situations of an increasingly destructive nature. Their removal will come about as a result of magnetic field energies of such frequency that they will be unable to continue their existence here. The *Space Intelligence* (positive extraterrestrial sources) wish it to be known that they are ready and willing to assist humanity in every way open to them at the moment of change, and also afterwards, as the planet is required to go through a cleansing period. Many of these *visitors* come from the fourth-dimensional universe, and have monitored the planet and its civilizations in the past.

In May 1969, a geologist, magnetic scientist and world authority on spacecraft thought that our *Space Brothers*, working through what some investigators are calling *Space Commands*, are using the *sensitives* of this world to direct messages of information in regard to dangers we are facing by the abuse of our atomic findings.

Therefore, it behooves the investigators of today, as humanity begins to move into the fourth-dimensional universe, to pay heed to the voices of these *sensitives,* who are able to record the apparent directives of these organized *Space Intelligences.* We ask that you do not discount this, but with an open mind inquire into it. This cooperation is possible because these *beings* have found the way to get from *their* planets to our own. They do it by the thousands all over the planet, day-after-day, week-after-week, year-after-year.

Seeing Our Spiritual Self

How are these "sensitives" able to communicate with *Space Intelligence?* Many begin to develop this *sensitivity* by seeing their *spiritual self* through meditation; a process of learning proper rhythm based upon cosmic life force. True meditation is the quieting of ones nature in order to become alert to dimensional frequencies beyond our own. These *sensitives* become aware of the Godhood, or true nature of the universe.

According to the *Space Intelligence*, it is good to set aside a period of time each day to "commune" with the spirit; a going within to truly find ones "self." This inner awakening is a natural process on the evolutionary path, and brings with it the reality of who and what we are destined to become. Our spiritual and physical natures are related; one is dependent upon the other. But to a greater extent, we are now opening to our higher spiritual nature instead of focusing primarily on our physicality. This most certainly leads to a greater perception and use of our talents and abilities. According to my extraterrestrial *source*, individuals in the distant past began to perceive their Higher Self, or Godhood, but mistakenly erred in thinking they had broken certain codes of behavior, when exactly the opposite was occurring. Although appearing as physical, their own Higher Self emerged as a luminescent being in a much finer and more subtle state. It is this same *emergence of the spirit* that is once again happening to humanity. Many individuals have recognized this luminescent being as a part of themselves that gives guidance and direction and expanded knowledge that others also inhabit our universe. We are again at a crossroad. Will we, as before, suppress this emergence of the spirit out of our own self-induced fear of the unknown? Or will we welcome this opportunity for inner awareness and allow it to occur? As our consciousness expands, we begin to comprehend that our Higher Self is there to help us; it is our gatekeeper, guiding us to experience other realms of existence. Therefore, it would do us well to acknowledge and become sensitive to that guidance and direction as we begin to explore the universe within us and around us.

CHAPTER FIVE
VISITORS OF ANTIQUITY

Historical Periods and Probable Dates

To our present knowledge, the North American continent in ancient times did not glory in the later golden cultures of the Mayas, Incas, and Tiahuanacans, yet its people can lay claim to a great antiquity. The caves and mysterious mounds found all over the mid-eastern to southern regions of North America testify to the humanoid remains discovered, along with the bones of animals.

The discovery of a fossil imprint of a sandal near Delta in Utah startled American geologists, as located inside the imprint were two tiny trilobites dated before the Cambrian Period, the oldest or earliest of the Paleozoic Era - about 250 million years ago! In 1866, a Professor J. D. Whitney found the famed *Calaveras humanoid skull* at a depth of 130 feet in an auriferous deposit. This was buried under lava more than twenty million years ago in a Tertiary Period layer on the western slope of the Sierra Nevada in California. Though these events would be enough to shake ones assumed attitude regarding the antiquity of man in this part of the world, yet another piece of evidence was discovered in a carboniferous layer in Cow Canyon, Nevada. It was the imprint of a humanoid foot stamped in clay of the Mid-Tertiary (twenty million years old) era, long before man was accepted as being present!

There is also the amazing find near Eureka, Nevada of what appears to be fossilized human tibia embedded in quartzite. In 1899 at Nampa, Idaho, Mr. M. A. Kutz was drilling a 300 foot deep artesian well through layers of soil, lava, quicksand and clay. Among other objects being sucked up through the pump, Kutz was startled to find a tiny female figure only one and a half inches tall. This figure was made from a plastic appearing material which was baked or burned with fire. The iron-oxide which cemented the quartz grains on the figure indicated that this tiny image dated from early Quaternary times, being the work of a very advanced culture.

An Early Dynamo?

In 1971 on a deserted beach area, an amateur anthropologist, Mr. Jack Kershaw, of Chico, California, discovered a truly startling find in a lava encrusted rock strata. It was found to be an authentic COMPLEX ENGINE dated some 50 million years old! According to Kershaw, he was fishing on a flat rock and saw some big waves coming in. As they receded, he saw the glint of something like copper. As an anthropologist, he at first thought the object might be an American Indian artifact. It was obviously some kind of motor. It has been looked at by the experts at Stanford (Stanford Research Institute) and in Washington, DC (perhaps by Georgetown University or the famed Smithsonian Institute). It turns out that the device was a motor with its own built-in power source.

According to Kershaw, the motor was about an inch and a half long and an inch and a half in diameter. The portion that stuck out from the lava rock was circular. It had four copper coils on both sides. The copper had not oxidized, even though it had long been exposed to salt water. There was also a hollow shaft running through the device between the copper coils. This shaft still retains magnetic powers. Both sides of the shaft repel at one end and attract at the other.

Kershaw had the device examined under a holograph—an x-ray machine that took photographs of the device, layer by layer, to show how it was constructed. Not only does Kershaw believe in its age of 50 million years, but Dr. Peter Stauffer, who was at Stanford University's Earth Sciences Department during that period of time, estimated the rock strata to be at least this old. According to Kershaw, the device has been estimated to have once produced up to 5 horsepower, more than any engine of its size today. There is no apparent technology to make a motor like this. The power supply pack is made of multiple layers of ceramic wafers about 1,000th of an inch thick. People have theorized that the device is actually a stabilizer or gyroscope from a flying vehicle, possibly even a spacecraft. What puzzled Kershaw and others who have examined it is that if this thing has been around for at least 50 million years, where did it come from and who made it?

East Indian Spaceships and "Vimanas"

In an era that was contemporary with both the legendary continents of Lemuria and Atlantis in approximately 21,000 BC to 14,000 BC, the following events were taking place in the Far East. There are many stories of so-called spacemen, flying discs, aerial cars, chariots, and celestial cars found throughout many manuscripts in ancient times. These appear to be almost contemporary with each other in the civilizations of Sumer-Akkhad, Babylonia, India (Hindu), Thibet (Tibet), Cathey (China), Yamato (Japan), Cambuja (Cambodia), and even among some Indian nations in the North American continent. There are also links to what now appears extinct civilizations which once flourished in both the Pacific and Atlantic oceans, referred to in our times as Lemuria (Muror), and Atlantis, Aztlan, or Altlantes (The Old Land). These links have been discovered in the manuscripts of civilizations of Mu or Egypt, the Sumer-Akkhad, Babylonia, and the Hindu-Southeast Asian and Japanese, which have come down to us in translated form in our present time.

There is also the contemporary former colony and present civilization of Hellas (Greece, Crete and Rhodes), which speaks of many "gods," who in translation could be those of a very advanced race of extraterrestrials of superior knowledge and powers from our own solar system, or even beyond into other areas of space.

We begin with the following references in history from ancient manuscripts in India, as well as a modern book on ancient East Indian aircraft:

39

"Rama, an ancient Prince of India, and his lady, Sita, were living in a forest when she was abducted by Ravana, one of the giants who fought and opposed Prince Rama (the Child of Light), whose father was King Dasartha, (a descendant of the solar race who ruled then in India and much of Southeast Asia and Japan). Sita was discovered on the island of Sri Lanka (Ceylon) by the Lord of the Mons-Khmer, who lived in Angkhor Wat (Cambodia), whose name was later deified as Hanuman, The Monkey-God." (Note - when you remove the prefix AN, meaning anthropoid or monkey, you have **hu-man**!)

"During the flight to Sri Lanka in the *celestial car* of Ravana, they came under attack by one Jatayu, in a GIANT BIRD (presumably similar to a fighter plane of today). After imprisoning Sita in a fortress on Sri Lanka, the Lord Hanuman flew across from India to the island and gave a token of Rama's to Sita. Rama then gathered a great army, and aided by the celestials (aerial forces), he launched an aerial assault, which caused Ravana to flee."

"Then a great and prolonged aerial battle took place between Rama and Ravana. Rama finally launched a Brahma's death weapon of celestial fire (missile?) and vanquished his enemy, Ravana. Afterward, Rama took Sita home in his celestial car, which was fitted with several rooms for passengers and crew, and the windows were fitted with flags and colors. It emitted a melodious sound which could be heard on the ground below. This celestial car was called 'puspaka' or 'pushpa' car."

The following poem is from another Sanskrit translation describing how many suitors from all over India were contending for the hand of the Princess of Panchala, Draupadi:

"And the gods in cloud-borne chariots came to view the scene so fair, bright Adityas (pilots?) in their splendor, Maruts (trainees?) in the moving car. Bright celestial cars in concourse sailed upon the cloudless sky."

Again, from another part of the same manuscript:

"Bright immortals, robed in sunlight, sailed across the liquid sky, and their gleaming cloud-borne chariots rest on turrets high."

In another verse:

"And he saw in them embodied beings of the upper sky, and in lotus-eyed Krishna saw he highest on high."

Further on, we read:

"Devas from their cloud-borne chariots and Ghanddavas from the sky gazed in mute and speechless wonder on the human chiefs from on high."

Spacecraft in ancient times are also mentioned in what is termed the Parvas, as in the following:

"...exceedingly resplendent like a celestial

car, O King, in the battle between the gods and the Asuras in the days of old, it displayed a circular, forward, backward and diverse other kinds of motion..."

"...Innumerable iron balls also, O King, then appeared like resplendent luminaries in the clear firmament.[10] Shataghnis, (crafts), some equipped with four and some with two wheels and innumerable maces and disci with edges sharp as razors and resplendent like the Sun also appeared there."

The following is an ancient description of a spacecraft as it sat upon the ground:

"Beholding that mound like a mass of antimony with countless weapons falling from it, Drona's son was not at all moved."

There is also a translation regarding aeronautics described in a work entitled, *A Manuscript from the Prehistoric Past* (Bhagadvatham). This appears to have a bearing upon spacecraft engineering in ancient times.

"In this book in eight pregnant and captivating chapters, the art of manufacturing various types of aeroplanes of smooth and comfortable travel in the sky, as a unifying force for the universe, contribute to the well-being of mankind, that can go by its own force like a bird on earth, or water, or in air. That which can travel in the sky, from place to place, land to land, or globe to globe, is

---

[10] See present reference to small intelligently-controlled metallic spheroids sent out by larger craft!

42

called 'Vimana' by scientists in aeronautics."

"The secret (technology) of constructing aeroplanes, which will not break, which cannot be cut, will not catch fire, and cannot be destroyed. The secret of making planes motionless. The secrets of hearing enemy planes. The secret of receiving photographs of the interior of enemy planes. The secret of ascertaining the direction of enemy planes approach (radar?). The secret of making persons in enemy planes lose consciousness. The secret of destroying enemy planes (beam weapons?)."

"Just as our body, if complete in all its limbs, can achieve all things, so an aeroplane should be complete in all its parts in order to be effective. Commencing from the photographing mirror (electronscope?) underneath, an aeroplane should have thirty-one parts. The pilot should be provided with different materials of clothing according to differences in seasons, as prescribed by Agnimitra."

"Three varieties of food should be given to pilots, varying with the seasons of the year, as per Kalpa-Shatra. Twenty-five kinds of poisons which arise in the seasons are destroyed by the above changes of diet. Food is of five forms, cooked grain, gruel, paste, bread and essence (fluids). All of them are wholesome and body-building."

"Metals suitable for aeroplanes, light and heat-absorbing, are of sixteen kinds according to Shownaka. Great sages have declared that

43

these sixteen metals alone are the best for aeroplane construction." [11]

Here is a translation in a modern interpretation from an ancient Tibetan manuscript.

"The glorious sun enchanted the earth to splendor inspiring the giants with the joy of life, the thrill of basking in the beauty of this wonderful world, living almost forever like the golden sky gods. Sunbeams danced on the wavelets washing this Tibetan shore and caressed the crowds sporting on the beach; children played and splashed in the sea, pausing to stare wide-eyed as a gleaming VIMANA glided down towards the gilded towers of Lhasa, the celestial city, whose translucent temples and flowery parks reminded the Venusians of their own fair planet." [12]

Soon after this idyllic period the earth was struck either by an errant aerobolide from elsewhere in our solar system, or by what could have been some type of super-weapon. In either case, we again quote:

"The foreboding of this catastrophe was soon confirmed. The nations on earth mobilized to withstand this shock. Shelters were tunneled into mountains and stocked with provisions and equipment for those few who did survive. The ancient wisdom was secreted in time capsules; *space-fleets from Venus rescued the chosen...*"

---

[11] See melds of graphite and metal or stealth.
[12] See Thibet reference to civilization of YU (Yeu).

"The world defense chiefs met with those of the *Jupiterian Council* to assist in leading a space armada to disintegrate the on-rushing monster with nuclear missiles; the distortion of spatial time-field tensors fused the electronic navigational devices and most of the fleet was wrecked."

What was left of this once Golden Age of Wisdom and beauty upon the celestial island was now found to be but a lofty plateau appearing to be thrust into the clouds, ringed by giant mountain peaks; the once proud remains of the buildings of Lhasa now mired in mud. This was also the period of the final battle of the Titans, or GIANTS IN THE EARTH. The sacred books of Dzyan mention the *Lhas* or ancient Asiatic Spirits having built the celestial city called *Lhasa* on the legendary island in Central Asia. This celestial city was inhabited by "Sons of God," who dominated earth and sky with great wisdom. Tibetans still believe that before the Himalayas appeared, their country was flat and fertile, surrounded by sea and peopled by survivors of the original sunken continent of Mu, Empire of the Sun. Once again the survivors applied themselves to the Gods to aid earth, and a few *extraterrestrials descended in their ships of light* to again teach man the arts and civilization.[13]

The Chinese have long held beliefs in celestial Gods, often depicted as riding dragons or wheels of flame (this also appears in Japanese art). They, too, probably originally worshipped *wondrous beings from the sun* rather than the physical sun itself.

The Japanese "contact" man, the Honorable Yusuke J. Matsumura, recalled that a personified sun was called a golden god in India, while the Chinese classics SHI-CHI and HAN-SHU have a description of the "golden colored heavenly man" who had been heard of as long as 500 years ago,

---

[13] See references to discoveries of beings called "Dropa" plus "discs" whose meaning is still unknown in Thibet.

between the age of the Han Dynasty and that of the Tang Dynasty. It is very significant that they used not "god", but "gold-coloured heavenly man."

Models of Cosmonauts, "Dogus" in Japan

In prehistoric tombs of Japan (like Chipusan) are found strange clay figures of curious little people called "Haniwa." These terra cotta figurines called "Dogus" from the Jomon Era appear to be of Caucasian appearance, not always of Oriental Mongol. Many of the archeologists at one time believed them to be ceremonial figures used in certain early rituals. However, their resemblance to many paintings of presumed "spacemen" found in other areas of the earth have now led to a re-examination of these figurines, and more particularly since the sending of our astronauts and cosmonauts into space. It is now suggested that these little men are wearing spacesuits and helmets. Again, the renowned former UFO investigator for Japan, Mr. Matsumura, and his learned staff of the Cosmic Brotherhood Association (no longer operating) had made a most thorough study of the Jomon figurines. In one convincing study, it was noted that the Tohuku area statues appear to be wearing "sunglasses," while those in Aomori Prefecture apparently had helmets and what appear to be diver's suits that resemble our American astronauts. These figurines have been dated at some five to seven thousand years ago.

In another area of the islands of Japan is located a most famed and revered tomb called Chipusan. It is found in the suburbs of Yamaga City, Kuamoto Prefecture, Kyushu. One finds a wall painting dated at about 2,000 BC showing an ancient Japanese king holding up his hands in greeting to welcome SEVEN SUN DISCS! This is very similar to prehistoric murals found in Etruria, Italy, India and Iran. Another of the pictures depicts seven people holding hands in a very large circle, looking upward at the sky and evoking the UFOs to appear. Archeologists had assumed such scenes were merely symbolic of sun-worship, but in light of extraterrestrials, this new look at the figurines now suggests that these resplendent orbs may represent spaceships. This would indeed revolutionize our concept of the past. The word "Chipusan" in the pre-Ainu (aboriginal language and culture) is said to have meant *the place where the sun came down.*"

In Japan, it has been shown that there is perhaps a strong connection between their "sun-discs," both winged and wingless, and the "sun discs" of ancient Egypt, Iran and Israel. We might take note that many of the major nations in the world do make use of wingless symbols on their aircraft. Dr. Yoshiyuki Tange stated in the magazine for the Cosmic Brotherhood Association: "It was found that those Sun Marks drawn inside ornamented ancient tombs in Kyushu are the symbol of 'flying saucers' thousands of years ago. In the meanwhile, a legend of the Ainu people in Hokkaido says that Okiku-rumi-kamui (ancient Ainu god) descended from the heavens and landed at Haiopira in Hokkaido aboard a shining *Shinta* (Ainu cradle), on which we discovered the same Sun Mark. He had taught a righteous way of life to the Ainu people, and destroyed an evil god (authors note: this is shown in an old painting of an evil bird being pursued by a fiery 'eight-spoked Wheel of the Spiritual Path'). *He* was a space brother himself who visited from outer space aboard a flying saucer."

Finally, the Japanese book called *Nihongi* reports that a Celestial Dog or Tengu of modern Japanese superstition is a winged creature in human form with an exceedingly long nose, which haunts mountain tops and other secluded places.

Egypt Had Them, Too

Did ancient Egypt also have visitations from spacemen? Could some of the unusual and strange events surrounding the Exodus of Moses and his people be answered by an *extraterrestrial* intervention in the lands of the Nile? A badly decayed papyrus was found among the papers of deceased Professor Alberto Tulli, at one time the

47

Director of the Egyptian Museum of the Vatican in Rome. The decayed papyrus was translated by Prince Boris de Rachewiltz and identified as a part of the Annals of Thutmosis (Thutmose III) circa 1500 BC. (Authors note: According to the works of Immanuel Velikovski, this event occurred much later or about circa 900 BC).

Those who have made a study of the field of ufology would at once recognize the resemblance of this apparent creature to spacemen mentioned in classical cases, and which are alleged to frighten ordinary citizens in the nations of the world in our present times. It can be pointed out that there may have been "landed spaceships" during biblical periods among the so-called sacred mountains where "angels" summoned the Prophet Moses to receive divine revelations. The exceedingly long nose of the winged creatures in human form may have referred to some headpiece with breathing apparatus. To some extraterrestrials, our type of oxygenated atmosphere could be very dangerous, even poisonous. We are reminded of the so-called super-being, OANNES, whom the ancient Sumerians thought of as a FISH-GOD, as he appeared to arrive striding from the waters of the Tigris-Euphrates River. Therefore, this *being* may have been wearing a spacesuit that resembled a type of "strange fish," except that the face, hands and feet were visible. The suit was described as having protuberances which contained these appendages. Perhaps one of those witnesses had a reason to create a superstition that might suggest that such manifested appearances in the mountains of Japan were fairly regular surveillance of these "children of the sun."

According to an ancient papyrus scribed by the priests of the House of Life in Khem (Egypt):

> "... In the year 22, of the 3rd month of Winter, sixth hour of the day, the scribes of the House of Life found that there was a 'circle of fire' coming from the sky...it had no head. From its mouth came a breath that

stank (ozone?). One rod long was its body and a rod wide, and it was noiseless. And the hearts of the scribes became terrified and confused, and they laid themselves flat on their bellies."

"They reported to the Pharaoh, and His Majesty ordered that those priests of the House of Life search their records as to the cause of this strange event. Therefore, the report was examined. The priests reported that nothing of this type had ever been seen before. The Pharaoh thought upon what should be done as he was meditating on what had happened, as is recorded in papyri of the House of Life. Now, after some days had gone by, behold, these *things* became more numerous in the skies than ever. They shone more than the brightness of the sun, and extended to the limits of the four supports of the heavens. Dominating the sky was the station of these fire circles. The army of Pharaoh looked on, seeing him in their midst as he stood between their wheels. Thereupon these fire circles ascended higher in the sky towards the south. Fishes and winged animals or birds fell down from the sky. A marvel never before known since the foundation of this land! And the Pharaoh caused incense to be brought to make peace on earth, and what happened was ordered by the Pharaoh to be written in the Annals of the House of Life."

A King in Sumeria Takes To The Sky

It is also reported that as the Pharaoh Ramses II was pursuing the Israelite Prophet Moses and his people across the parted waters off the neck of the Sea of Reeds, his army

49

was witness to a most startling sight. They were to report that they saw their Pharaoh swept up by a large water spout.

> "And they all fell upon their faces and were sore afraid of what they all saw, and they thought they would never see their King again in this life. And they turned about and returned to their Capitol, Memphis, and there they were all astonished to see their Pharaoh continuing to rule over his people!"

Here we are left with an enigma as to just how the famed Pharaoh Ramses II, the former adopted brother of Seti-Meshu (Moses) survived the incident of the "water spout" in which his chariot was literally "lifted upward." To all purposes, that should have brought an end to his pursuit of the people of Israel. But instead, almost miraculously, he was found back in his palace in the capitol, Memphis. What indeed was the water spout? Could this have been a spaceship causing the water to form a whirlwind due to its magnetic field? Who or what were the personages *Osiris, Isis, Horus, Thoth,* and many other well-known early historical rulers of Khem or Egypt? In reality, could they also have been spacemen and spacewomen?

Mention of this period following the Antediluvian flood showing descent of spacemen and communication between earth and other areas of space is found in the Sumerian King-list. In an historical book entitled *Ancient Near Eastern Texts* relating to The Old Testament, translation is given of the popular legend of Etana, who apparently consorted with spacemen! The introduction notes make this statement:

> "After the Flood, Kingship was lowered again from heaven. In Kish (Ur), Etana, a shepherd, he who ascended to heaven and consolidated all countries, became King and ruled 1,560 years (Dynasty)."

50

Cylinder seals of the old Akkhadian period depict a figure by the name of Etana—a mortal in all respects, except that his name be written with the determinative for "God," a usage applied also to Kings of the old Akkhadian and some of the succeeding dynasties and the subject of an elaborate legend:

> "Etana had been designated to bring to mankind the security that kingship affords. But his life was blighted so long as he remained childless. The one known remedy appeared to be the plant of birth, which Etana must bring down in person from heaven. The difficult problem of the flight to heaven was eventually solved by Etana's enlisting the aid of an eagle. The eagle had betrayed his friend, the serpent,[14] and was languishing in a pit as a result of his perfidy. Etana rescues the bird, and as a reward is carried by the eagle on a spectacular and fitful flight."

The Babylonian eagle, or Simorgh, was well-known to be associated with the gods; it is not clear as to the significance of the serpent, except that it was often a symbol for a wise man. Perhaps the legends conceal an historical incident wherein a king ascended in a space-ship to another planet. A rather startling version is given by Alberto Fenoglio in the Italian magazine regarding UFO's, *CLYPEUS*, Anno., III, N.2, presumably quoting from Ur, Assur and Babylon by H. Schmoekel, translated as follows:

> "...excavations in Nineveh, there was discovered in the Library of King

---

[14] See reports of an eagle clutching a serpent in Mexico, and in the Yakima Valley, Washington, USA.

Assurbanipal clay cylinders on which is described a voyage to the sky. It narrates how King Etana, who lived about 5,000 years ago, called the 'Good King,' was taken as an honored guest on a flying ship in the form of a shield, which landed in a square behind the Royal Palace, rotating, surrounded by a vortex of flames. From the flying ship alighted tall, blond men with dark complexions, dressed in white. Handsome as gods, who invited King Etana, somewhat dissuaded by his own advisors, to go for a trip in the flying ship; in the middle of a whirlwind of flames and smoke he went so high that the earth with its seas, islands and continents, appeared to him like 'a leaf in a basket,' then disappeared from sight."

"King Etana, in the flying ship, reached the moon, Mars and Venus, and after a two-week absence, when they were already preparing a new succession to the throne, believing that the gods had carried him off with them, the flying ship glided over the city and touched down surrounded by a ring of fire. The fire abated, and King Etana descended with some of the blond men who stayed as his guests for some days."

This piece of remarkable translated text does appear to evoke the experiences of Enoch, Ezekial and the more recent 'contactees' George Adamski and Eduard 'Willy' Meier.

Dragons, Spaceships and Fish Gods

Many fired clay tablets on tiles, which have been unearthed in Babylon, depict flying dragons—the symbols of spaceships used by the Chinese. The Babylonians believed that God existed in the "sea of space" and the Jews prayed to their "Father in Heaven." All antiquity worshipped the supermen in the skies. Initiates of Babylonian Mystery Schools often styled themselves as "Sons of The Dragon," meaning originally "Disciples of the Spacemen." Ugaritic poems referred to Baal, Son of Dagon, as "Rider of the Clouds." He was believed to have a wonderful place on a lofty mountain in the North, similar to Solomon's Temple. (Authors note: Recall that tribe in Northwest Africa, who for centuries have held in reverence an area in Barnard's Star region as sacred. They could even describe its appearance, yet had never observed same because they had no telescope with which to do so! They called their tribe "Dagon." Spacemen may be called "Riders of the Clouds." They, too, are said to approach from the North through vents in the Van Allen Belts).[15]

Once again, we have a translation about a mysterious spaceman alleged to be some kind of deified "Fish God" (Authors note: Again the similarity to the ancient deified Fish God "Dagon") as reported by historian Alexander Polyhistor:

> "Berossus describes an animal with reason, who was called OANNES (John); the whole body of the animal was like that of a fish, and had under a fish's head another head, and also feet below, similar to those of a man, sub-joined to the fish's tail. His voice and language was articulate and human, and a representation of him is preserved even to this

---

[15] See ancients "North or Power" open to the North

day. During the day, this *being* conversed with man, but took no food at that season; and he gave them an insight into letters and sciences and every kind of art. He taught them to construct houses, to found temples, to compile laws, and explained to them the principles of geometrical knowledge. He made them distinguish the seeds of earth and showed them how to collect fruits; in short, he instructed them in everything which could tend to soften manners and humanize mankind. From that time, so universal were his instructions, nothing has been added to the material by way of improvement. When the sun set, it was the custom of this *being* to plunge again into the sea and abide all night in the deep, for he was amphibious. After this there appeared other animals like OANNES."

This historian, Polyhistor, then continues:

"Beroussus wrote concerning the generation of mankind, when there was nothing but darkness and an abyss of water. Men appeared with two wings, some with four, and two faces, organs of male and female."

In another fragment of the same type of material, Abydenus stated:

"A semi-daemon (demon) called Annedotus, very like to Oannes, came up a second time from the sea. Then Davs, the shepherd, governed for the space of ten sara (Authors note: a sarus = 3,600 years, a dynasty); he was of Pentibiblon. In his time, four double-shaped personages came out of the sea to land, whose names were Evadocus, Evirigames, Ennebolus and Anementus."

In what is considered metaphysical terminage, the use of "sea" or the "deep" often meant "regions of space." A creature with a fish's head and another head underneath and human feet appears to have been a man wearing a spacesuit! The reference to androgens with four wings and two faces seems vaguely suggestive of Ezekiel's famous sighting by the river Chebar, and probably refers to spaceships, not to spacemen themselves. In our present time period, we have numerous reports of spaceships plunging into our seas. Therefore, Oannes, like Neptune, could actually have emerged from the sea or even very deep rivers. It was written that the Lord Jehovah retired to the Tabernacle every night and so Oannes returned to the "deep," and we presume his spaceship.

CHAPTER SIX
THE HEAVENLY HOSTS

"They (the sanctified ones) come from a far country, from the ends of heaven."

--Biblical quote

Myth or Legend?

As Solomon said so long ago: "There is nothing new under the sun."

The author would add: "Knowledge brings continual change to that which was once new; therefore, what was once new, through change and time, is eventually rediscovered. Mankind might learn through this that it has the choice NOT TO REPEAT what was once used to destroy what had been conceived, indeed, as NEW."

There are many individuals today who report they have been visited by strange *beings* whom they claim are presumably from the regions of outer space, or from other more removed solar systems in far galaxies. Even the famed seer of the 16th century, M. Michel de Nostradame, once penned a quatrain in a famous letter to his then sovereign King of France, Henry de Valois, Second, to the effect that:

> "And in this last era, all the kingdoms of Christianity, and also of the unbelievers, shall quake for the space of years; there shall be more grievous wars and battles; towns, cities, and castles (buildings) shall be burnt, desolated and destroyed with a great effusion of vestal (pure) blood; married women and widows ravished; sucking babes dashed against the walls of towns, and so many evils shall be committed by the means of the

infernal prince, Satan, that almost the entire world shall be undone and desolate."

"Before these events, many unusual birds (possibly UFOs or Heavenly Hosts) shall cry through the air "huy, huy" (now, now). A little while after that, they shall vanish. After this shall have lasted a good while, there shall be renewed a reign of Saturn and Golden Age. God the Creator shall say, hearing the affliction of his people, that Satan shall be tied and put in the bottom of the deep, and there shall begin an Age of Universal Peace between God and man. Ecclesiastical power shall return in force and Satan bound for the space of a thousand years."

As it was in the days of the famed Biblical prophets and seers, it appears that as we have come to the end of the Piscean Age and into the beginning of the Aquarian Age, we still have the Heavenly Hosts making contact with those who have chosen to answer the present call to spiritual awareness. But perhaps we should set some precedents for such events in our own era and time by giving further examples from past history on earth. There are writings, hieroglyphs, and carvings dating back into prehistoric antiquity that speak of, or depict artifacts, of what appear to be both spacecraft and their intelligence.

The Indians of North America, for example, still repeat today an ancient story which the poet Longfellow immortalized in his poem *Hiawatha.* It is the story of Red Sun, who was also like a sun that descended to earth and brought the Son of the Evening Star, who created humanity.

"And they picked of them wives, every one which they chose, and begot *men of renown, men of eald* (old)."

Many scholars and writers believe that the Grecian and Roman god of both Olympus and Fiesole were in reality space intelligences whose supernatural powers could have been nothing more than super-scientific in nature. They believe that such tales go back untold thousands of years to when these space intelligences came to earth to create and nurture the race of people who may have been here (beings such as Zeus and Chronos). Perhaps a team of these intelligences *did* land, led by someone who became the ancient representation of Zeus (Jupiter) due to brilliant engineering skills in electrical forces (legendary hurling of bolts of lightening). This might also account for what has become known to us as LASERS, RACERS AND MASER BEAMS. It has also been shown that Zeus brought with him such illustrious beings as Mercury (perhaps a god of communications, particularly computers) and Saturn (Chronos, known as the Ancient One with the Scythe, or Father Time). It is alleged by others that the planet Saturn is the "hub" of government, although in *another time-zone* of this solar system, called by the *Space Intelligence* "Salon Three Koldas." Saturn-Chronos was the father of Zeus-Jupiter, and therefore, a type of supernal god of gods. There was Neptune (possibly a type of underwater craft commander) called Triton, with a famed four pronged symbol of power rising from the bowels of the watery depths to lure and harass unwary sailors to a final resting place. Apollo was a being considered to be a true oracle or "teller of the future" and likened to some helio-sun god or Phoebus-like idol. Then there is Mars (Ares or Eros), who it appears may have had a background in mechanical engineering and volatile chemical forces. This Mars being seems to be a catalyst for more subtle forces of nature; thus at times considered to be fiery or passionate.

Now comes the female *space intelligence*, such as the goddess Venus (Aphrodite-Demeter). Venus may have been an ancient representation of the so-called "mother goddess" and came down to us in a somewhat garbled version as a "love goddess." It was Venus who truly represented the basic building block for life as we know it, the DNA factor! Then there were Athena-Minerva (Nike) and Hestia, the sisters of Hercules and daughters of Zeus-Jupiter, who were reputed to have great strength to withstand forces of evil, as well as to right the balance of wrong-doing—exhibiting Christ-like powers. And we should not forget Pandora, daughter of Zeus. She was represented as containing many secrets of science, as well as that which could destroy the life process if ever unleashed. It appears that it was from their heavenly unions with mortals of earth that they may have begotten a race of giants who were *mighty upon the earth in those times.*

There were also those symbols which may have clearly delineated the descent from the sky, such as the LION for its strength and nobility. The GRIFFONS bird-like head (when appearing as an eagle-headed griffon) was known for its wisdom and intelligence, as well as its tenacity, and the halo of the giant ORION conveyed that he brought down sun powers or sources of powerful energies. What of Jason and his crew, who sailed the ship Argo? Could this have been some type of space ark? In light of today's understanding of UFOs, it could be interpreted as a huge spacecraft with a large crew of many Jupiterean (Olympian) space intelligences. It was also a Russian writer on outer space who through archeology brought to our attention that in the Biblical *Apocrypha* (an early scriptural writing) the "Star of Bethlehem" moved about in a strange fashion, as though not a star. This premise was banned by the church fathers as being heretical. In light of certain facts today, there is the possibility that the Star of Bethlehem might have actually been a space vehicle! It hung over Mount Vans for a whole day and once alighted on the mountain "like an eagle." The text, written by early Christians, further claims that it appeared Christ came down from a Star!

It was discovered a few years ago that a famed monastery in Yugoslavia called the Dechany had frescos dating back to Byzatine times of the Holy Eastern Synod.

These frescos most vividly depict flying objects remarkably similar to early satellites. These also depict the interiors, even to its control machinery, at which sit several astronauts. Yet these beings are still today listed as "angels" or "saints" without the slightest sign of haloes or flowing white robes. It is as though these messengers of the spiritual life were *not* divine creatures at all, but highly intelligent, god-like appearing *Hosts* from advanced worlds in our cosmos. Isn't it possible then that the ancient Biblical "angels" were really missionaries from spiritually and technically mature civilizations?

Again, the Holy Bible is perhaps among the richest source of statements regarding the Heavenly Host, or possible *Space Intelligence*, as the following might attest:

> "And Moses went up into the midst of the cloud and got himself up into the Mount." (Exodus 24:18) "And the Lord descended in the cloud..." (Exodus 34:5) "And the Lord went before them by day in a pillar of a cloud..." (Exodus 13:21) (Pillar could be understandable as a cylinder or large type of carrier craft). Isiah said, "Who are these that fly as a cloud and come as doves to their windows?" (Isaiah 60:8)

It was also stated that the Master Jesus took three disciples up unto the Mount of Transfiguration (meaning to be transformed from one appearance to another). There He appeared before them in His *Glorious Light Raiment* as He stood discoursing with a presumably deceased Moses and Elijah, who the disciples clearly saw as not dead, but still living. Upon their utterance of praise and building Tabernacles for these three great teachers and prophets, a mighty voice spoke out to them in a commanding tone, both chastising and exhorting them to hear the teaching of this great Messenger of the Lord God. As these disciples departed the "cloud" which sat upon the Mount, they

60

stumbled as if in a daze. (Authors note: not unlike many experiencers who have likewise "stumbled as if in a daze" when encountering a UFO). The disciples were then told by Jesus to say nothing to the villagers below of what they had seen that day upon the Mount.

It was much later that Jesus suffered the ignominy of the Crucifixion and was resurrected into life from death. Before this took place, He dispensed His gifts unto His disciples. When He had done so..."Behold, when He had spoken these things, while they beheld, He was taken up and a cloud received Him out of their sight." (Acts 1:9) (Authors note: Jesus appears to have entered the "cloud," disappearing from their sight, and ascending into the heavens). The Apostle Paul later wrote that it was impossible for human flesh to be assumed into heaven spiritually—only a spiritual body may be assumed spiritually into heaven. We may well wonder what it was then within the confines of that "cloud" which lifted Jesus up. Could it be the same "cloud" that will return in our Aquarian Age, as written in prophecy, to bring back the Lord of Light in all of His glory together with the Heavenly Hosts in that great day of spiritual and physical renewal? It is written:

> "Prepare you the way before the Lord! Make straight the highways! For the Lord shall come in the CLOUDS with great power and glory, and every ear shall hear Him, and every eye shall behold Him. And the trumpets shall be sounded, and there shall be a lull in the heavens for the space even unto half an hour. And then shall there be a great and tumultuous noise upon the earth. And then shall the Lord descend upon earth in a cloud, and the Heavenly Host shall cry out; now is the time that our Lord is come and *they*, together with the heralds, shall sing Alleluia, Alleluia, Alleluia. There shall be joy unbounding, both in heaven and upon the

earth, for the Lord of Lords, King of Kings, the Prince of Shiloh, is even in our midst, and all the stars of morning shall sing together!"

Other Lives—Other Planets

Could it be possible that *we* are the descendants of the biblical "space travelers?" And if so, could we have at some time lived an existence on other planets? This is certainly possible, according to the *Space Intelligence*. Our existence on any world is for our growth and potential as individuals, as each inhabited planet has its own opportunity for experience and learning. We are reminded that the Master Esu stated, "In my Father's house are many mansions. If this were not so, I would not have told you."

My extraterrestrial *source* states that once an individual has finished an incarnation and has returned to the spiritual dimensions, they may in time find the need to return to the physical in order to carry out the balance of that which remains on their life record. However, there may be a difference in time and light energy from one realm to another. For example, a year in earth time may be as 100 years within the spiritual dimensions. A soul is always guided by those great ones within the spiritual realms as to their record of incarnations, letting the soul decide when to take up embodiment once again to carry out tasks which would add a perspective of growth and potential. In some cases, there could even be an *exchange of soul identities* which has been termed "walk-ins." One soul walks out; the other soul walks in. According to my *source,* this walk-in arrangement could even involve an intelligence from another planet who has the need to experience life in that particular circumstance, or has volunteered to the exchange in order to help a planetary system in times of need. The *Space Intelligence* assures us that all is in a given order in the cosmic plan of life.

A Message to Star People: Their Tasks

Presently, there are many of us who are awakening to the knowledge that we have genetic roots going back into the far reaches of antiquity, and not necessarily confined to planet earth. We are gaining understanding that those we consider "alien" could very well be our distant relatives. "Star People" is a designation given to those persons who have agreed to incarnate at this time to help awaken others to this knowledge. Those who have begun this awakening process seem eager to reconnect with other beings in our universe. Here is what my *source* says regarding "Star People…"

> *We (Space Intelligence) speak to those who have the awareness of being in service to others. This is the most important task and purpose that you carry out on behalf of the Solar Confederation. Seeking inquiry of your connections to those who exist on other worlds is to some degree important. However, in our dealings with earth individuals, there is less emphasis on recognition of what is beyond your planet, for there will come a time when the 'Mission' will be accomplished and many will return unto their sources.*

> *You (Star People) have a Universal Identity and are connected to others who exist in space, but to those who seek out such connections, we have stated, "To apples we salt, we return!" Therefore, you are upon that world (earth) which is likened geophysically to an apple. You have been "salted" upon your world, just as have many others, and have taken up incarnation to learn, to reason, and to be of assistance. There are many areas*

of your heavens from which those of other worlds have come to your planet - those of the Pleiades, the Dal Universe, Epsilon Eridani; Tau Ceti, near Acturus; Coma Bernices (Virgin's Hair); those of Lyra; Cicumpolar Cap; Ursa Majoris; Austrinis Pisces (Southern Fish); Zeta Reticuli One; and Alberio (Northern Cross). There are literally millions of beings who are represented by those who travel the corridors above your planet and those who are under the Solar Confederation. You do have connections with these beings and this is for your knowledge.

One should make a study of tongues going back to its beginnings through those nations which were very ancient upon your planet. Those who dwell in that nation you call the Peoples Republic of China and Nationalist China; those who dwell in the nation called Japan; those who dwell in the nation called Espana, particularly in the Pyrenees mountains, who are termed the Basques; also the ancient language and writing in hieroglyphic form of those of the Ural Mountain area or the Caucasus, and those of that nation you call Egypt; those of that nation you call the Baath Republic of Syria (Syriac language). These all have unusual written forms of language which derive from pictographic or ideographic depictions.

Studying the meaning of these ancient writings will begin to unravel what took place or existed before the building of the Towers, Ziggurats or Pyramids, just as that individual called Proscourioff deciphered the Mayan glyths and writing during the late 1980's,

64

uncovering its secrets in recent times. There was also a man by the name of Champolleon who discovered the Rosetta Stone, which he used to translate the ancient Egyptian hieroglyphics. Study of ancient tongues and ancient writings is tedious work, and could take a lifetime. The DOTS on these ancient manuscripts denote emphasis or give special meaning to a word or glyph. Thus, it may change the intonation of a word. It is similar to the Micronesian-Polynesian tongues one would find on the Pacific Islands.

A History of Earth

According to the *Space Intelligence,* there have been others from beyond our earth who have walked our planet during the Pre-Cambrian and Cambrian Era (250,000,000 B.C.). A record of this has been found in solidified, fossilized sandal footprints discovered throughout the ages. Civilizations going back several tens of thousands of years are found in ancient mythology in various lands; further information can be located in the Hindu works and writings found in India and Tibet. I am informed that contact with *Space Intelligence* reaches as far back as the ancient continent referred to as Gondwandland.[16] It was one of the largest existing land masses during that early period. Eventually, out of the breakup of this land mass, the ancient civilization of Lemuria was formed. The Lemurian continent consisted of what are now the South Pacific Islands up to the western edges of the Asian continent, including the sunken man-made stonework found recently near the Japanese Ryukyu Islands (Yanoguni). It also included the Japanese Island chain prior to their present landmass. This was referred to in *Space Intelligence* records as the "Lotus Land"

---

[16] Gondwandalnd was made up of what is now New Zealand, Australia, Japanese Islands and Antartica.

which broke up into portions and sank beneath the ocean depths. Other mountainous locations formed through volcanic actions, which are today above water and form the South Pacific Island chain. Some of these Islands contain descendant survivors of the result of sidereal warfare referred to as the "War of the Titans." This warfare brought about vast upheavals, which affected not only the Pacific locale, but also caused atmospheric changes, glacial advances and volcanic eruptions. Entire civilizations became extinct, such as the Atlantean and its vast colonies in what is now Spain, Ukraine (Urals), Egypt, Greece, Ireland, Great Britain, Malta, Azores, South America, and the north and northwestern African locations.

It was during these early times that the earth was visited by an extraterrestrial race known as the "Saturnae," who were of a more scientific-spiritual cadre. Upon their departure, a different *Space Intelligence,* referred to as the "Jupitereans," arrived just about the time of heated differences between the Atlanteans and Lemurians. The Atlanteans were known as the Children of One, or On, and were at one time very spiritual. However, the Atlantean priests had gradually begun to revert from an enlightened spiritual path to a more animalistic, corrupt path referred to as Belial or Baal. Their differences finally erupted into an internecine sidereal (atomic) war.

Just as in those early time periods, our planet continues to be visited by many different extraterrestrial *Space Intelligences;* those who are presently observing us have taken note of our preoccupation with violence, bloodshed, and internecine battles between our nations. This is the continuance of the wars of the Sons of Light against the Sons of Darkness, which I am told is inscribed upon an ancient script. From the perspective of those *Space Intelligences* who now observe, we of the earth appear at the point of either entering into an era of peace, or extinguishing regions of our planet by use of sidereal weaponry, which has proven to be a terrible example of the misuse of our civilization's greatest talents and abilities. These *Space*

Intelligences are in hope and work diligently to guide us toward a peaceful solution and a final conference where a peace document can be agreed upon by presently warring nations. *They* continue to await the outcome, reminding us that there have been many practices and teachings sent to earth, but the real truth remains the same. A Diamond is a Diamond, yet would shine forth from its many facets the Light of Truth.

Cubes, Bell-Shapes and Recording Devices

We have established that it appears more than probable there have been visitations and outright contact with both spaceships and their occupants, the ubiquitous extraterrestrials, down through almost forgotten corridors of time stretching into the dim and misty past. There may also be other evidence that strongly lends itself to the establishment of a more advanced culture or science from ancient to present times. There appears to be unimpeachable evidence from findings which were both unintentional and those which were thought to exist and then uncovered. Perhaps we should begin with the strange "cube" uncovered in a German coal mine in the year 1865. The cube was found deeply embedded in a layer of earth dating from the Tertiary Period (approximately 20,000,000 years ago). In 1886, Dr. Gurlt, who was the original discoverer, made this find public. In several other publications and works on the subject, especially the Academy of Sciences, it was stated that the mysterious cube had two slightly rounded opposing faces, and measured about two and a half inches by one and four-fifths inches, the latter measurement taken between two rounded surfaces. The cube weighed about twenty-eight ounces. A fairly deep incision went all the way around about midway up its height. Its composition was that of hard carbon-nickel steel and it did not contain enough sulfur to be made of pyrite. Many experts said the object was artificially manufactured. It was deposited in the Salzburg Museum, and as time passed there was less talk about it. By the year

1910, it no longer appeared in the museum's inventory. But where did it go? After the Second World War, even the file relating to that period when the cube was at the museum had disappeared.

The magazine, *Scientific American,* had reported many stories of this type before the turn of the century, including one that appeared in (Vol. 7, page 298, June 1951). According to the account, a metallic bell-shaped object measuring four and a half inches in height, six and a half inches in base width, two and a half inches at the top, and having a thickness of one-eighth of an inch, was uncovered when a solid rock was dynamited. The object was made of a metal resembling zinc, but from its description it sounded like a silver alloy. It was concluded that the object was of considerable antiquity; the rock that had been dynamited was itself several million years old. The object circulated from museum to museum and then disappeared. It has not been found since.

One may wonder why such unusual objects are found and what, if anything, they might be used for on our earth. It is more than possible that at one time these may have been highly perfected *Data Collectors* of the same type as a magnetic band. There have been calculations made on the possibilities of a Data Collector made of iron and having the capacity of a human brain! These results have been surprising. We could assume 100 percent efficiency in data storage and retrieval, and duplicating the contents of a human brain would require an iron cube with 2.10^{17} atoms. Put another way, one-thousandth of a millimeter, or smaller than the head of a pin. One hundred percent efficient cubes or parallelepipeds, measuring several hundred centimeters per side, could store the most highly detailed data on every-thing that had taken place on our planet during the last ten million years! The data could have been fed to these *Collectors* by radiation, of which we were unaware, and

---

[17] 17 zeroes following.

which scanned our planet like radar. If this were the case, then perhaps some day these *objects* will no doubt disappear from the museums just as the Salzburg cube disappeared. Perhaps they will have been retrieved by the *intelligences* who placed them on the earth. In my opinion, this is far from science fiction. The hypothesis follows a far too logical line of reason. If some of the life on earth was artificially modified, the experiment must have been followed up, and from time to time the extraterrestrials must have been able to retrieve the "recording devices" that had been placed on the earth during the length of some seventy million years since their experiment began. Perhaps even more interesting will be the discovery of one of these objects having "magnetic fields" on which we might find stored data on the periods prior to the appearance of Homo Sapiens.

The reason I believe such *objects* will eventually disappear is based upon the recent contact cases in the nation of Switzerland since the year 1975. These took place in the beautiful Alps region of that country to a now well-known gentleman by the name of Eduard "Willy" Meier. Mr. Meier appeared to have been picked because of his intelligence and interest in the subject of spaceships and extraterrestrial life in the cosmos. In one of these "contacts" with beings from what had been given as the Pleiades in the constellation of Taurus, Meier was given what purports to be some type of strange metal. This metal was turned over to a former scientist with the business firm of IBM in the United States and was placed under scientific scrutiny and analysis. The result was most unusual. It was discovered that the metal was not only an amalgam of metal and crystal, but contained several other "unknown materials!" However, the possession of this object was very short-lived. Shortly after its examination, it disappeared from the guardianship of the scientist, and to this day has never been seen again!

Babylonian Batteries--Energy, Electricity

In the years 1938-1939 near the Iraqi city of Baghdad, a German archeologist by the name of Wilhelm Koenig discovered a number of earthenware jars with the necks covered with asphalt. Inside the jars were iron rods encased in copper cylinders. Herr Koenig described his discovery in *9 JAHRE IRAK*, which was published in Austria in 1940. He thought they were electric batteries from ancient Babylon. What? Electric batteries in ancient Babylon? This surely needed further corroboration. But this corroboration did not occur until after World War II, when Mr. Willard Gray of the General Electric Company created a duplicate of the 3,060 year old battery, filling it with copper sulphate instead of the unknown original electrolytic material which had evaporated. The sister battery of that ancient Babylonian vase-shaped cell was tested, and it worked! Thus, it was conclusively shown that the ancient Babylonians *did* use electricity. With his team, Herr Koenig also uncovered some electro-plated articles in the same general area. It can safely be assumed then that one of the purposes for the batteries was electroplating![18] Similar jars were also found in a shaman's (magician) home, but it is presumed that both priests and skilled craftsmen kept such knowledge as a trade secret. The electroplated materials have been dated at circa 2,000 BC; that is, they were 1,060 years older than Koenig's ceramic cells. Since electroplating and galvanization were introduced only in the first part of the nineteenth century, this again shows that a certain technological process used 4,000 years ago has been rediscovered in modern times! Since this area was the Babylonian Kingdom, we would be remiss in not again mentioning the possible *Extraterrestrial Oannes* who had brought the arts of civilization to the Sumer Empire. This may have been one of the technical products of the arts which Oannes brought back to the artisans during that period, and was no doubt lost after the time of the

---

[18] See pre-Incan electroplating in Peru circa 13,000 B.C.

Deluge (about 9,600 BC). These very same devices may have been used in Egypt, as Professor Denis Saurat found evidence of such devices in that ancient land. It then became almost a common discovery in many ancient countries and cultures. Many of these devices could be termed "perpetual lights" as they burned for centuries in sepulchers and mausoleums of those of wealth or royalty and in temples of archaic ages.

CHAPTER SEVEN
MODERN-DAY VISITATIONS

Adamski; Historic Visitation, 1952

No outline of this type would be complete without more recent incidents of *contacts* of both spaceships and extraterrestrials. We would begin with the now famous case of Eagle Mountain and the "Venusian contact." Mr. George Adamski (deceased) was a metaphysical philosopher, teacher, student and "saucer" researcher. In 1952, his home was in Palomar Gardens, California, on the slopes of the famous Mount Palomar. An avid student of the heavens, Adamski had a deep belief in life elsewhere in the cosmos. He was also a gentleman that my wife and I considered to be a dear friend. He seemed not only to understand our feelings about the spaceships and their occupants, but was very compassionate regarding our purpose in communicating the information we were receiving from our *Space Intelligence Source* for other individuals upon our earth. In any case, George Adamski had worked toward the purpose of one day actually standing face-to-face with those who came in their flying saucers, and even to being taken aboard. He was to finally reach this goal in the fall of 1952.

It was late August when Adamski received a visit from Mr. and Mrs. Al Bailey of Winslow, Arizona. During the course of a private conversation, the Baileys told him about Dr. and Mrs. George Hunt Williamson of Prescott, Arizona. It appeared that these four individuals were as interested in "flying saucers" as was Adamski. They claimed to have made "contact" with the occupants of "saucers" through ham radio during the years 1950-1952. After Adamski met all of them, they asked him to call when he made the next attempt at "contact." Adamski kept his promise. He called Dr. Williamson on the 18th of November, 1952, to tell him that he and the others should meet him at a location just outside the city of Blythe,

California on the morning of November 20. Adamski also took along his secretary, Lucy McGinnis, as well as Alice K. Wells, the owner of the Palomar Gardens Café. It was just after 8:00 a.m. that the group met and proceeded toward Desert Center, California, turning on the highway that went north toward the town of Rice, California. Adamski suggested stopping the car at a particular spot along the side of the road and getting out to look around. He would decide what they should do at that point.

It was about 11:00 a.m. when they reached this spot and they spent about a half-hour examining the flora and fauna in the area. A short distance away, they noted a shallow wash bed which seemed to come down from the end of the mountain ridge to its base. The wash base then continued to wind its way between risings on the side of the road where they were roaming about. Curiosity overcame Bailey and Adamski. Leaving the others, they walked across to the base of this ridge to see what was on the other side of the mountains. They discovered that it was similar to what they had already seen on their side, except for the highway which extended for many miles. Shortly after noon, they heard the sound of an approaching plane. As it passed overhead and continued its line of travel, they simultaneously turned as one, looking again toward the closest mountain ridge where just a few minutes before the plane had crossed. There, riding high and without a sound, was a gigantic, cigar-shaped, silvery spaceship, devoid of wings or other appendages. It appeared to be drifting slowly. The craft came in their direction, then stopped, hovering motionless.

"Is that a spaceship?" Dr. Williamson asked excitedly.

"No, George, I don't believe it is," Lucy replied. She was schooled in caution against undue excitement and quick conclusions.

"That baby's high, and see how big it is!" exclaimed Al Bailey.

"And it doesn't have wings or any other appendages like our planes do!" persisted Williamson.

Before Al Bailey could answer, Lucy interrupted, "You're right, George. Look, it's orange on top—the whole length!"

In the excitement, Alice Wells asked Adamski to get his telescope and camera out of the car and take a photograph of this unusual craft. Betty Bailey was so excited she could not get her own movie camera set properly before the strange looking craft began to move again. However, they were able to use the binoculars they had brought with them. All had a good look at this "odd airship." It was with the binoculars that George noted a dark marking on the side of the craft which appeared to be some type of insignia, but he was unable to make it out in detail. Adamski knew in spite of all the excitement that this was not to be the place, maybe not even the spaceship with which they were to make contact. But he felt this huge craft had a definite "something" to do with it all.

Once again in their car, and after receiving an impression that they needed to get to a less noticeable spot, Adamski and the rest of the group looked up and saw the large spacecraft also turn and move silently along with the car. The craft was now high in the sky and looked to be about halfway between the highway and the mountain ridge. They had driven approximately a half-mile on the dirt road when Adamski noticed another rough road to the right. He asked Lucy if she could safely turn onto this path for a short distance in order to get closer to a spot which he felt would be ideal for setting up the telescope. It looked as though this road might be on the ground directly under the big ship.

The road was strewn with broken bottles and glass; nevertheless, they succeeded in making it safely to within 200 feet of the spot Adamski had chosen. Here the large ship appeared to be almost directly overhead. When the car stopped, the ship also stopped! They quickly unloaded the equipment and set up the telescope as firmly as possible. Adamski told those with him to go back to the car with the others, and for all of them to watch closely for anything that might take place. Adamski then asked them to return in an hour, unless he signaled for them before that time. He explained that when the saucer left, if it did come in as he hoped, he would then walk back to the car.

While Adamski had a desire to meet with an actual occupant of the "saucer," expectation that it would actually occur was far from his mind. However, he did hope to get some good pictures of the craft, particularly one with close-up detail. About five minutes had elapsed when his attention was attracted by a flash in the sky. Almost instantly, a beautiful small ship came into view. It appeared to be drifting through a saddle between two of the mountain peaks. It settled silently into one of the coves about a half-mile from him. It did not lower itself entirely below the crest of the mountain; only the lower portion seemed to settle below the crest. The upper, or dome section, remained above the crest in full sight of the rest of Adamski's party, who were back down the ridge watching. Adamski spotted the ship in the finder of his telescope and camera. As quickly as possible, he snapped seven rolls of film without even focusing properly. His hope was that luck was with him and the pictures would turn out well. The saucer flashed brightly as it moved away and disappeared. At that time, a couple of Air Force planes roared overhead.

Adamski wondered who was piloting the beautiful craft and wished he could have a chance to talk to the pilot, maybe even look inside the craft. Suddenly, his train of thought was broken as his attention was called to a man standing at the entrance of a ravine. The man stood between two low hills about a quarter of a mile away. He motioned for Adamski to come to him. Being certain that the man had not been there before, Adamski started toward him, mentally questioning who this man was and where he had come from.

As he approached the man, Adamski felt a strange feeling come over him. He became cautious. He looked around as though to reassure himself that he was in full view of his companions. The stranger looked like any normal man, although somewhat smaller than Adamski and considerably younger. There were two outstanding

75

differences that Adamski noticed as he neared him. The man's trousers were not like Adamski's - the style was much like ski pants. And his hair was long. It reached to his shoulders and blew in the wind.

Adamski proceeded on foot toward the strange person. Suddenly, he felt as though a veil had been lifted from his mind. The feeling of caution was now completely gone. By this time, he was quite close. The *being* took four steps toward Adamski, bringing them within arm's length of one another. Now for the first time, Adamski fully realized that he was standing in the presence of a man from space—*a human being from another world!*

Adamski goes on to narrate what further took place on that eventful afternoon of November 20, 1952, and that he subsequently received another visit from the spaceship at Mount Palomar on December 13, 1952. Other visitations followed, and finally journeys outward into space and to another planet in *their* solar system. Possibly, Adamski may have been put through a process to allow for time-travel into *their* dimension, where the real planetary life and civilization exists for the parallel solar system to ours.

Eduard "Willy" Meier and the Pleiadians

At present, there is a great deal of controversy surrounding the now world-famed experiences of Eduard "Willy" Meier and the "Pleiades Contacts" in the nation of Switzerland. Willy Meier's first experience of actual physical contact with the inhabitants of the area called Pleiades began on January 28, 1975. However, according to Meier, his experiences started much earlier in his life, as his first sighting of a UFO occurred on June 2, 1942, when he was only five years of age. Meier claims that during that same year he was invited to "take a ride" on a peculiar pear-shaped UFO by an "odd-looking man."

While spending time in India during the early 1960's, Meier observed and photographed UFOs on several occasions and began developing what he claims as telepathic communication with their occupants. His first "contact" at that time turned out to be a female cosmonaut who informed him that they came from the DAL Universe. He was also informed that her people were several centuries ahead of the technology and sociology of the Pleiades, but were very cooperative and closely associated with the Pleiadians. She gave her name as *Asket* (pronounced As-kot). She had strong features, very similar to blond-haired, fair-skinned Nordic types.

According to the book *Breakthrough* (Lancer Books ISBN 79324175), Mr. Meier was making an attempt to receive voices on a tape recorder on the afternoon of January 28, 1975. Although his first result was weak and inconclusive, voices could definitely be heard. It was during a second attempt that he was successful beyond expectation. A definite message told him to take his camera and go outside. He took his camera, went outside and got on his Mo-Ped. He had no idea where he was going, but appeared to be guided by an inner voice. It was about 1:00 in the afternoon. After driving through the Hindiwill-Schmidruti village, he came to a field, then drove through meadows and forests, finally stopping in an open glade-like area.

The time was now 2:14 p.m. Meier had been driving for over an hour when he heard a peculiar whirring noise. Looking up into the cloudy sky, he noted an object that shot out of the clouds, then slowed down and arced almost the length of a football field away. The object was disc-shaped with a raised dome and extended base. He took several pictures before it disappeared. Climbing back on his bike, Meier sped away towards a woods to the east and a boggy clearing in the forest. He then walked about another 60 yards, laid down his bike, and noted again the whirring noise and the reappearance of the object. He took several more pictures. Just then, the object began to land on the meadow. Meier ran toward it in order to observe it more closely. However, he states that he ran into a "force-field" of some type that prevented him from moving forward. Sitting down upon the grass, Meier stared at the disc and waited.

He did not wait long. From behind the object, a figure appeared. There was no doubt that this was a female in a very peculiar suit, similar to those used by USA astronauts. Meier stated that the suit was more like a close-fitting coverall of an unusual greenish-gray color. A ring ran around the neckline of the suit, presumably for fastening a helmet. Meier noticed that the woman had long, reddish-blonde hair, as the helmet was not in place at that time. Obviously, our atmosphere agreed with this cosmonaut from another world. She appeared to be friendly and without pretension, as though she had a naturalness without an attitude of superior abilities. She radiated self-confidence and natural grace. The female came closer to Meier, taking him by the arms and pulling him to his feet. Her grip was strong and self-assured, but pleasant. Together, they walked very slowly to his bike and sat down on the dry grass. The woman began to speak in perfect German with a peculiar accent. (Not Meier's own home language, but one that he understood close to his Swiss-German).

Their discussion lasted for quite some time, and it developed that the occupants had put out a "force-field" around the area of the contact of approximately 175 yards so that no one, or no thing, could come closer than that without being stopped. He further found out that her name was *Semjase* (Sim-yas-e), and that her home planet's name in the Pleiades was *Erra* (Air-ra). She informed him that their terrain was similar to that of the lower Swiss Alps. Semjase stated that they had been planning this trip for some time and wished to develop a "voice channel" for earth's humanity in order to assist humans to come out of centuries of misunderstandings. A great deal more was developed from their conversations.

Although there has been much controversy in the ensuing years regarding Eduard "Willy" Meier and his contacts with Semjase, who is to say that it *did not* happen? It seems that often, when someone comes forward with personal "contact" stories, there are those who would immediately dismiss these encounters as nothing more than an "overactive imagination," or worse—a type of mental imbalance on the part of the experiencer. In my opinion, Willy Meier's experience in 1975 was one of the most important and perhaps vitally imperative "contacts" ever made upon our earth.

We have discussed two well-known cases of contact with "other worldly" beings and their craft. However, there are literally thousands of lesser publicized cases circulating throughout the world. Go to any bookstore and you are likely to find a variety of books on the subject of UFOs, ranging from scientific research to personal experiences. From all walks of life, ethnic backgrounds, and belief systems, people who have had these encounters are beginning to come forward; to speak their truth, even though they may be ridiculed by others who have not experienced such visitation. In bringing forth this information, these experiencers are hopeful of creating an awareness that we have *always* been visited, observed and mentored by enlightened beings who reside throughout the cosmos.

In my own association with *Space Intelligence*, I have requested from them explanations for several commonly asked questions. Following is the information given. The words in parentheses are my own clarification.

What Type of Propulsion Do These Spacecraft Use?

The methods that drive our spacecraft would be far more technical than you could understand, but basically it is Phase Fusion Energy (magneto-solar) of a certain spectrum rating through that which is a form of created crystal or crystalline matrix (laser crystals?). This is done through certain forms of "super conductivity." That is, the energy is held in place by certain methods which provide great entropy (energy constant) or potential (continuing flow of energy). This is emitted through certain coils and condensers which

79

encircle the spacecraft or whatever is to be operated within a frequency field. As it passes through flux (magnetic fields about a planet) it is bent back to its origin or point of emission. This operates in perpetuity within a timed cycle, or what you on earth refer to as "perpetual motion." We also have back-up batteries which are used in the event of an emergency.

Our craft then continue to operate through certain resonant fields (one level of magnetic field). As the energy is pulsed and in harmonic, we create that which assists us in reaching vectors, spatial parsecs and sectors in the heavens. Because these craft are capable of being vectored to a given point in space and time, and that which has been artificially created as a balanced horizon heading, we are able to head toward that point and from point to point.[19] Just as your earth operates with as little as four gauss, our spacecraft operate with greater gauss (magnetic force or impulsion) per square inch, as we traverse through space. The field operating our spacecraft (harmonic pulse in resonance) can then be increased as a mass unit (mass energy X speed, divided by time/distance), or "stepped up." This can affect the immediate space or environs and could be dangerous or hazardous should another object or individual come too close in proximity. However, such fields also assist in deflecting any or all substances which may accidentally or deliberately come into contact

---

[19] UFO's are often seen to zig-zag or move erratically.

with our spacecraft. Therefore, we adjust these fields when disembarking or embarking, when allowing others from your planet to come aboard, or when we take onboard biological subjects or materials needed for research.

We do not authorize the filming or televising of our people (extraterrestrials). However, our spacecraft are allowed under our rulings to be visually seen and filmed, as they do not portray accurately those of our people who are our crew or those in command of such spacecraft. If many of our people were filmed or televised, then those who would walk the avenues of your planet could be set upon or otherwise placed under peril, not only by earth inhabitants, but by governmental individuals and agencies of many nations of your planet. Therefore, contact continues so long as filming is not brought up as a request by those contacted, or even as verification of such contacts. There is also a further reason why we are not filmed. This is due to a difference in Time Differential or Dimension in which your film is not capable of retaining an image, even though we appear to be just as physically visible as those of your planet.

Do the "Space People" Know God?

We, Koldasians, who dwell beyond the time barrier, have a physicality of the same level of that in which you exist in your embodiment; the so-called physical level. We are well-aware of the appearance, energy and the love from that which you term Almighty

81

God, Father of Lights, and His Illustrious Son, Jesus the Christus, the anointed One, the Messenger, the Teacher of Righteousness. Thus, we commit fully to this! It is imprinted upon us, and within our spacecraft. It is Ageless Life and Light, and we deal both through, of, and by that greater Light!

We are in your understanding very ancient, for we came upon your planet many hundreds of thousands of years ago, and set forth to build a civilization in love, peace and joy. Unfortunately, the mixture between the aboriginal earth race, or primeval, and those races of exiles placed on your planet by the Solar Confederation, were such in their breeding that this created genetic differences. Finally, through time, this developed five distinct races. We of "Koldas Salon Three" are made up of three races.

We are those you termed "angels," or Ang-les...that which came by way of a ninety degree right angle. It is mentioned in your Scripture that John, whom you called The Revelator, was "taken up" and stood before the building referred to as the "Palace of the Sea of Burning Glass" (location of the Four and Twenty Elders or the Solar Tribunal/Solar Council/Solar Government). John "fell down as though to worship the angel he had seen come out of the Sea of Burning Glass." The angel said unto him: "See that you do it not; worship God only."

The solar system we are referring to, in which the above building is located, is known as Salon Three, inhabited by those people who once inhabited your own solar system but were forced to evacuate due to implosion of that planet called Maldek. Our solar system is in a parallel universe, which places us in an entirely different time-space dimension.

When Are People Taken Onboard UFOs?

We do not make the decision as to when people are taken onboard UFOs. It is entirely by the direction of our Elders, and is dependant on whether you are at a point in your learning process, enlightenment, and understanding to be ready for such an experience. One may be taken for the purpose of increasing their knowledge of this field, or for learning of those who are in your atmospheric levels, and of those who arrive and depart from your planet. Therefore, we make no arbitrary decisions as to an individual being taken onboard our ships. It would depend greatly upon whether there is a need to be carried out, or whether by doing so you would be any better served than others.

Are Beings Sent to Earth, Banished to Earth, or Are They Volunteers?

The only purpose for individuals being banished to earth would be as an exile, or one who has committed errors which are grave or which have caused many to lose their existence. This would be a way of atonement if carried out on your planet. However, all have existences of creation, and all are part of that same creation which is sent forth from that energy source; that which is constant and is still connected. Therefore, all are sons and daughters of Ageless Life, Our Radiant One, Almighty God, Father of Lights.

When one considers that they have been "banished," then they are punishing self for whatever purpose, and they need to perhaps seek out some insight into mental problems, depression, or a lack of self-esteem. An individual, by the very act of incarnating on the earth, is to carry out specific purposes which are placed in the record and have been accepted by the individual. In dealing with this upon your planet, one does at times arrive at points of opposition or seeming obstacles. However, Almighty God, Father of Lights, always considers that this Source creates the proper methods by which to meet each and every obstacle, so that the individual is capable of dealing with same, placing this behind one's self, and getting on with life. All is energy in movement. An obstacle is but a momentary interruption in this energy. It is termed "unrewarding reality." Therefore, it appears to be somewhat difficult—a challenge to overcome. An individual is greatly loved by Almighty God, Father of Lights, and should not continue to denigrate against ones self, or consider ones self to be less than that which is light and love in expression—Almighty God.

Each individual needs to learn that they are truly loved and understood, and to deal with those matters that appear to be obstacles from within, through strength, experience and hope, and through supplications (prayers) to overcome each and every challenge set before you. Make use of your higher nature, your spiritual Godhood. Did not the Master Esu long ago state, "Know ye not that ye are Gods?" Therefore, be about your Father's business and get on with that which is your life.

Giant Rock Convention - 1967

Shadow of UFO over Giant Rock Convention 1959

Giant Rock after closure in 1978-79 by San Bernadino County and FAA

October 1967 just to the east of Blue Rose Ministry.
Rev. Shirley Short was told this UFO in its ionization
screen would appear. The UFO formed on the northeast
of a hill of granite; then moved behind it and appeared
again on the southeast.

UFO over Giant Rock, CA. Convention, 1959

CHAPTER EIGHT
ORDINARY PEOPLE—
EXTRAORDINARY CONTACT

Positive Extraterrestrial Contacts

According to the *Space Intelligence*, positive contacts are to encourage and assist individuals in a positive manner to achieve certain goals and results. My *source* states that these positive contacts are *not now* and have *never* been intentionally forced upon us, but function only as encouragement. Some contacts take place every seven years in our time by reason of change in our system of bodily functions; the number seven is considered a *sacred numeral*. I am informed that those contacts which proceed beyond *seven times seven* (7 X 7) or *forty-nine* (49) of our earth years are for the process of spiritual enfoldment. It is hoped by the *Space Intelligence* that we will come to understand the main purpose which they have tried to convey in their contacts with those of our earth. That is to *"serve your fellow being to the best of your ability, so long as this does not remove the bread from your mouth, or the mouths of your family."* The *Space Intelligence* remain in contact in order to encourage us so that these acts of service are carried out, although individuals oftentimes are not knowledgeable as to their periodic contacts or visitations for this stated purpose. It is also to encourage our scientific and logical exploration of the cosmos and, in particular, extraterrestrial life forms and their sciences and technology.

We are also advised to have a healthy skepticism of certain aspects of these experiences, and are encouraged toward investigation of extraterrestrial life forms or the *manner in which they arrive upon our world* (anti-gravitational fields and magnetic properties). My *source* states:

There are connections for all individuals who first CHOOSE US AND WE THEN CHOOSE YOU. As we have stated: "To apples we salt, we return." Therefore, we continue to make such exploration surveys or visitations upon you who are DESCENDANTS OF MANY OF OUR OWN PEOPLE who once inhabited your solar system.

Know that what you do on the earth planet is the most important task you will carry out at present. Therefore, that which you make use of to be of assistance to your fellow man to the best of your ability is stated simply. It is not complex. There is a connection with us, but you have chosen this incarnation to be of whatever assistance you might offer to those of planet earth. Be about this in everything that you do in dealing with individuals to give them insight and under-standing—the comprehension of life on life's terms. Those of you who understand this have learned to make use of that innermost self, that spiritual godhead. You have begun that journey, that pathway of directing your fellow beings, as well as yourself. Therefore, it is most important. You have entered your Father's House and He has laid before you the Feast of which you have chosen to partake (spiritual enlightenment).

Many of you have had past planetary incarnations which bear upon your present identity. Otherwise you would not be in-terested in this field of discovery and the investigation of UFOs and extraterrestrials. Nor would you feel associations with that of an extraterrestrial nature, were it not for that which has been a previous part of your function. However, think not so much for self, but to benefit those around you and those you seek out. As you do so, be very certain of your protection before you seek out inquiries regarding certain information pertaining to UFOs or other planetary life forms. Do not allow those extraterrestrials that are "outside" of the Solar Confederation to be of non-beneficial interference. We are not here to please or otherwise add to the egocentric personality of individuals on your planet. This includes those who receive such information from those types of other planetary sources. We are, in the main, making contacts to encourage learning processes and insight. As to self, this insight is either earned or deserved by that which you carry out on the behest of others on your planet, particularly those who are in need of your services, but oftentimes do not have what you term "earth credits" (dollars). Nonetheless, continue to serve such individuals. Assist those who have means, and assist those who are not able to pay for your services due to lack of funds. However, be discerning of the truth and honesty of such individuals in the matter of meeting your needs in assisting them. Understand that one may "entertain angels unaware." Those who seek you out for your assistance are often led to you by extraterrestrial sources with whom you have been in contact. Therefore, as you call forth to be of assistance or aid to your fellow being, you will gain potential which will grow by your efforts.

Remember, you produce work, then we (space intelligence) work, and together it works! We have given information and guidance to assure each individual that IT DOES WORK...IT DOES MANIFEST! It is brought forth by the works of each individual! Again, be humble and grateful in and for all the assistance you receive. There is, of course, a great deal more to work upon in the nature of individuals upon your planet, so that each might bring forth from within themselves that which would be STRENGTH, LIGHT AND LOVE; those aspects for which each individual will be the very epitome of what we have stated.

Early Childhood Contact

There are many upon the earth who claim to have experienced extraterrestrial visitation since childhood. The *Space Intelligence* explains:

There is a purpose for early childhood contact; to awaken you from that which has been but a physical part of your activity on your planet. It is done to start the process of a long search, seeking after that which is within you; that which is already known, already recognized, and already in operation. You are Gods in the making; that which has and will continue to come forth and light your path. Do not be anxious after this, for it should become apparent as you pursue it. You should become more positive in your aspirations and inspirations, so that in its finality, you would be a server. You would be one who would be a guider of other individuals who are in need of the same answers, or the same dynamism and positivism.

Early childhood contacts have occurred so that individuals will become more aware of their purpose and their connection to this. For this reason, we have appeared over your planet from time to time so that here and there people awaken. They may be drawn to us. And as they are drawn to us, we might communicate once again, "Serve your fellow being to the best of your ability." Be grounded upon the soil of your planet, responsible for your actions and what takes place with yourself insofar as its effect upon all around you.

As you awaken, you would then find beauty wherever you observe. There is that axiom among people of the nations, "To see in beauty and walk in beauty, let beauty go before you. Let beauty be behind you and you will walk in beauty all the days of your life." It is that which is the giving of yourself and your energies toward that purpose.

Early childhood contact may take place during that period from approximately seven to ten years. This is a very moldable period, where once you are aware of what is taking place, you should continue to walk in that path, and may never forget, never look back, but always forward, always upward!

We (Space Intelligence) have contacted individuals in early childhood who have taken up their embodiment in this particular time cycle to learn of others upon other worlds and their activity. These extraterrestrials are related not only to you, but to other individuals beyond your own world. Although you have little knowledge of these other civilizations that exist about you, they are observable within your time zone.

Early childhood contact has drawn you out of the so-called "cocoon" of your physical egocentric personality and into that which now says to you that you are a Spiritual God-Being. It has brought you to the awareness that you are in reality much more than you had presumed. This, in the main, is the reason for childhood contact.

Species, Clones and Humanoids

I have also attempted to elicit certain information from my *source* regarding some of the various extraterrestrial beings with which humans have come into contact. These beings fall into categories we might label *"species, clones and humanoids."* According to my *source,* "clones" are considered *pre-programmed intelligence.* They are different in physiognomy than humanoids, and are used to carry out explorations, surveys and other tasks which may be hazardous to humanoid species. They have an intelligence, but only function in certain aspects and have little emotional response. The function of these clones had been temporarily approved by those systems of the Confederation, based upon continuing observation of these entities as they carry out their tasks. If members of the Confederation observe that this program is a hazard to the occupants of other worlds, this approval is discontinued. The humanoids are then utilized in place of the clones. The clones are observed from Confederation craft, and although they operate somewhat independently, they are sometimes brought on board and placed under direct supervision. These *clones* will continue to operate unless destroyed by accident or intention in exploring other worlds they visit. They have a different life fluid (blood), and different sight and hearing faculties. In most cases, the laryngeal areas are unnecessary, and they are programmed to act upon telepathic instructions. Therefore, we might hear nothing more than guttural sounds instead of speech. Such types of intelligence are fairly common throughout the many galaxies and universes, and have gained technological knowledge by way of their programmed extrasensory abilities.

Many physical life forms in the cosmos do ingest nutrients to sustain their bodily functions. Water is one substance that they use. I am told by my *source* that their own populace from "Salon Three Koldas," through centuries of development and their evolvement in a different time zone and dimension, ingest a form of highly purified liquid or water. They realize that we of the earth have created a need to artificially purify our water supplies to avoid the forms of pollution which are created by our industries. This pollution rises into our atmosphere and can be found in our oceans, rivers and streams. Through the diurnal rotation of our planet, this same pollution may be spread throughout the world. My *source* further states that extraterrestrial scientific spacecraft have discovered particles in our atmospheric levels inclusive of nuclear waste, such as Strontium, Cesium and Iridium. This may be one reason why humans undergo a faster aging progression, whereby *Space Intelligence* from Koldas might live several hundred years. (Authors note: When encountered, these Koldasian beings look very healthy and appear no older than 35 years of age). Various dimensional and time zone factors must also be taken into consideration in the aging process, along with the suggestion that humans are born into a particular type of magnetic grid and molecular structure.

There are many variations of "species, clones and humanoids" who belong to organizations associated with or directly related to the Solar Confederation. However, there are those whom the Confederation refer to as "outsiders." These "outsiders" may be technologically advanced, with

95

major interests in biological and technological subjects, and only minor interest in sociological or spiritual sciences. These "outsiders" are mostly responsible for the physical examination and experimentation with life forms on our planet, often without permission of individuals, and in cases of animals, entirely without permission. However, at times, the Confederation will also examine animals due to the hazardous conditions that appear on many planets. My *source* states:

> *There are individuals who are associated with the Confederation who have traveled from the southern heavens. These are many and varied. These beings arrive over your planet following given navigational routes, and observe your planet for given purposes.*

> *Observation of one species by another species is common throughout the universes. There are many worlds that are in various stages of development, which you have come to know as Jurassic, Protozoic, Palezoic and Mesozoic, even as far back as the Cambrian era, where we have discovered what you term "prehistoric creatures." When possible, these have been taken aboard our craft for examination after being placed into a state of suspended animation, then released again on the planet where they had been discovered. The creatures upon such planets are still undergoing changes analogous to early time periods upon your own planet.*

> *Other species are considered crossbreeds or hybrids. These beings are used particularly for medical observation of their bodily and sensory functions and life cycle. This is done for the gaining of knowledge of how these*

individuals might be crossbred with other life forms in the universe. Unfortunately, many of these crossbreeds have met with transition or death, as they are unable to exist in such mode upon other worlds due to differentiated cardiopulmonary actions and atmospheric pressures.

There are some individuals on your planet who believe that the one you call Jesus could have been a special kind of breed, and the only one of his kind. However, if that were the case, what about other great teachers of light and truth, such as Siddharta Gautama (Buddha), Lao Tzu, Pythias, Origin, Ziusthusra or Zoraster, Seti-Meshu (Moses), Abraham, Lot, Joshua, Caleb, David, Elijah and Elisha, and many more. There _were_ given differences with each of these individuals in regard to the so-called normal mode of conception on your planet. There are certain key factors present in each individual who is in communication with our people, no matter what their present form, planetary world or parallel time field.

Life forms, such as the Iarga (E-Arga) people, are a species that create after their own in appearance. There are even mammalian creatures which create clones after their own. However, this is fairly rare and has only recently been discovered on distant worlds.

Many other planetary species are capable of changing their molecular fields. Therefore, when these beings appear to you, their energy appears to be of the physical. Though little

*known by your scientists, their physical basis
is carbon-copper. There are those beings who
are not necessarily humanoid in cycle, but
created. One might take note of peculiarity of
facial features, narrow nostrils or eyes located
behind large lens-appearing protectors. The
ears are not very discernible, and there is
peculiarity to the skin coloration. These types
of beings have been seen from time to time by
many of your earth people, and unfortunately
often cause fear. Later, when it is realized
they are not negative in their intentions, but
under command of those who are most
interested in your activities for a positive
purpose and constructive result, they become
accepted, and your own people comprehend
that they do not intend harm.*

*Not only are we, the Confederation, in
contact with humans on the earth, but
presently have made contact with those that
you refer to as "Sasquatch" or "Bigfoot" in
order to raise their level of intelligence.
These creatures are in need of developing in
your earth conditions, as they are of the same
life cycle. These "tall ones" can be highly
intelligent, but retain some animal factors.
They have the ability to communicate in their
own fashion, and when confronted, create a
condition preventing them from being
bothered or harassed by your species. They
are extremely strong and able to move very
quickly, taking in five to six feet in stride.
When hunted by curious humans, they
become fearful for their own life and emit a
shrill sound. This is a warning to all other
Bigfoot in the vicinity to leave or seek
protection, as a foreign type of intelligence*

has entered their area. In many cases, these Bigfoot are often seen within a short time after our craft have entered a given location. This may be in deserted higher altitudes on your planet, particularly in the Himalayas, the Kush, the Pamir, Frazier Park in British Columbia, and given areas of the West Coast of the United States, such as the Humboldt Range. Although little known, they also appear in the Alaskan range near Mount McKinley. Much of these areas is relatively unexplored and not usually visited by the outside world of your media.

These "tall ones" are remnants of a previous civilization on the earth. They were driven below the surface of your planet during certain geological upheavals which have taken place from time to time, dating back to the Poseidan (Atlantis) period. Their height will generally range from approximately six foot, five inches, to upwards of seven foot, six inches.

We were observing your planet even in the times that you consider prehistoric, when dinosaurs roamed the earth. Their gradual extinction was, to an extent, due to atmospheric changes from early aeriform fluid over your planet. This aeriform fluid greatly dissipated from a tropical or semi-tropical climate to a frigid zone. Much of their disappearance was also brought on by volcanic disturbances which vented poisonous gases into your atmosphere. There are still some of these prehistoric creatures in existence upon your planet. Such creatures disturb your scientists and their already established concepts of life forms from such time periods.

There are also various species in the universe likened to those "outside the Confederation" who have a type of nature that is like those of your earth—sometimes aggressive and warlike. They are interested in levels of procreation or regeneration. Therefore, they attempt to discover information through means which are otherwise unallowable by our Code of Law. Since your earth planet is not yet a full member of the Solar Confederation, you are not as yet under the Code of our protection. For this reason, you fall prey to those "intruders" now in your midst. Again we urge caution with such intruders and ask that you be discerning as to their appearance. Often these individuals wear apparel completely absent of color, or black. Some of these come from an area of the southern hemisphere of the heavens which is in proximity to a system that appears similar to the letter Y (see Grus - Southern Hemisphere of Heavens). This system's sun star would be rather dim by your measurements and its name in your equivalent language would be unintelligible.

There are recent reports of strange creatures in your more isolated areas, particularly in the east and southeast. Those that were reported were of amphibious or scaly appearance, possibly Draconians. Since their sight range is adaptable to night conditions, the eyes often look reddish, similar to your small canine or feline types. They appear to have a covering like a protuberance in the ear and nose areas. These are "filters;" not for breathing, but for a particular decibel range in sound. They have three to four digits on their hands and feet, and many are ambidextrous. These beings appear to many of your people very frightening. They are created creatures—clones—and are becoming adapted to your atmosphere by the "outsiders." There have been sightings reported in the area of Pascagoula, Mississippi, Oklahoma, Florida and many other areas.

Cloned beings have also been sent in the stead of other humanoids, who met with resistance or demise while attempting to create trade relations or technological and scientific exchange with those of the earth.The pre-programmed beings that are sometimes witnessed are used for scientific and biological explorations and are protected from certain elements within your atmospheric conditions. What you term UFOs make use of such types, as they are equipped with camera-like vision. When they disembark from our craft, it is for this purpose. Figurines from the Jomon era in your nation called Japan are similar replicas of these presumed robotic types. The outside covering is a lightweight suit of tightly bonded material which appears metallic. In the early Jomon era, these programmed types had moveable and removable wrist, neck, torso, head and leg areas. They also had a shield or goggles to protect the sight areas, and a type of "breathing tube" or umbilical cord connected to a back-pack similar to your own astronauts. Lastly, they had built-in antennae on top of the helmet. This type of being was also seen in your more recent time in that which is called the Alpe D'Italienne by a man whose name was Mongussi. These particular robot-appearing types function within a field effect; therefore, caution should be exercised in approaching too near.

There are many who have come forward on your planet with information regarding implants found in the human population. Many of these implants are done by those considered as "outsiders," and not part of the Solar Confederation. Very probably, those known as Orionites, who originate from a system in your heavens known as Orion's Belt that imploded in a Nova approximately eighty years ago in our time, may be the perpetrators of this implant program. These beings are known as "Greys." The implants are used in the same manner as those of your animal control scientists or experimenters in tracking animal life forms for their migrations, habitations and areas of birth.

We have spoken of a small number of "species, clones and humanoids" existing in your physical universe. However, there is much that exists about and around you of which you have very little awareness. Other dimensions exist side-by-side with your own physical third dimension, and with your thought processes, which is the fourth dimension. These other dimensions will become more apparent as you develop in your quest for understanding yourselves as universal beings. There is much that will open to the people of earth as you bring forth energy of the Aquarian Age into which you

102

have entered. You will develop into a race of
great beings, very capable in the use of your
mental and spiritual abilities.

Challenging Extraterrestrials: Are They of the Light?

How do we humans challenge extraterrestrials that may not have our best interests at heart? What protection do we have against these intrusions into our perceived "normal" life? These are concerns that are becoming important and necessary for us as a species to acknowledge. We cannot ignore anymore the evidence that tells us we are being visited, studied, and contacted by extraterrestrial entities. Again, here is what my *source* has to say:

As these contacts with extraterrestrials
occur, be very certain that they are of a
positive nature. You have every right to
inquire of these beings: "Are you committed
to Almighty God, Father of Lights, and his
illustrious Son, Jesus the Christus, and to the
enlightenment and service of other
individuals?"

If those to whom the inquiry is directed
give a positive response, well and good. If it
is evasive or unanswered, then it would be
better that you work upon this, surrounding
yourself with the greater light of protection.
Seek out those upon your earth who are of a
spiritual nature, such as those who work with
sources of light. We are deeply committed
and have been on your planet for many
thousands of years. Many of your people are
connected to our civilizations, but again,
always be very certain of such connections.

You of the earth are beginning a journey that will be of great inspiration, aspiration, spiritual comprehension, and development of your abilities. That is why you have begun to undergo these present experiences which so many of you have been having. We give to you a prayer which you might use in protection. Remember it well!

Adonoi, Adonoi, Adonoi,
Kadosh, Kadosh, Kadosh, Tavayot!

Adonoi, Adonoi, Adonoi,
Kadosh, Kadosh, Kadosh, Tavayot!

Adonoi, Adonoi, Adonoi,
Kadosh, Kadosh, Kadosh, Tavayot!

It is a prayer which has been said by great leaders and those who waged battles against those of the darkness in the past history of earth. If this space intelligence that comes to you has a belief in Ageless Life and Light, our Radiant One, Almighty God, Father of Lights, and is committed to serving the light of He, whom you call Jesus the Christus, or Master Esu, then this encounter has to do with Guidance or Purpose for you. If there is improper identification from these beings, then we would firmly state, "Begone, in the name of Almighty God, Father of Lights."

Gateway Through the Belt of Orion - A Warning from the Confederation

According to my source, we are warned to be careful in association with any factors dealing with that part of our heavens known as Orion.

It is from that area that interferers called "Greys" came from and have committed those acts (abductions) which shall be held accountable in the future for examination by Almighty God, Father of Lights. These particular beings are creatures of their own desires and have carried out experimentation not only upon your animal level, but also upon individuals on your planet.

There are positive and negative forces in the universe, just as there are positive and negative forces existing on the earth. In your quadrant of the universe, the Belt of Orion represents the gateway to duality. It is the area that gives energy to the egocentric personality; the duality and opposite of the Spiritual Godhead and true cosmic freedom. The area of your heavens representing the Spiritual Godhead is known as the Pleiades. As was said by Salome, the wife of Samuel of the temple in Jerusalem, Israel, "Oh, Master (Jesus) how long shall it be before the twain art one?" Jesus replied, "Verily, verily, I sayeth unto thee, woman, just so long as thou dost continue to bring forth in pain and travail, that long shall it be before the twain art one." Then said she unto Jesus, "It is good then that I have not borne children." Jesus rebuked and chastised her, for she understood him not. For he had said unto her that just so long as we continue to dwell and give energy and power to duality between that which is egocentric personality and Spiritual Godhood, one being of the gross flesh, the other being the freedom of the cosmos, then one limits oneself to flesh. Again, Jesus had said, "Though the spirit is willing, the flesh is weak." Therefore, flesh is but a temporary house for that which is the Spiritual Godhood, which you separate out of—like a schoolhouse for a learning experience to develop toward that which one is truly. A belief in duality is to continue to believe in death rather than life. That which is opposite of "evil" is "live" and that opposite of "devil" is to have "lived." That which is "love" is to "evol" (prefix of evolution). When the statement was made in your Holy scriptures, "Canst thou unbuckle the belt of Orion, or unloose the sweet influence of the Pleiades," these are references to nodal points in the heavens. One is representative of Godhood, that which is influential upon individuals in matters of sweetness and joy; the other representative of flesh and bone, or that which is girded about and limited.

It is only a misconception which long ago was created to separate the children from the Godhood; that is, to live out their desire rather than their need. This allowed the Godhood to experience the difference between Freedom and Duality. When we begin to lose hold of duality, we then enter the door of freedom. That which is representative of the door of duality has dual direction. One may either enter into a world of flesh and bone (physicality) or exit out of same and take hold of that which is the Sweet Influence issued forth from the Throne of Godhood (represented by the Pleiades).

(Authors note: John's statement about the 'little book!) It is sweet to the lips when one understands that one has a great influence in all that takes place within the cosmic scheme of life. But when one explores duality, it becomes as bitter as gall to the stomach. To exit the door of duality is by way of complete surrender and acceptance of spiritual Godhood.

CHAPTER NINE
VOICE FROM SPACE

A Factual Account of a Warning to Earth

The following pages contain reprinted material from what I consider one of the most important and startling documents ever revealed to our earth planet in our times. I do this with grateful thanks to the following publications and individuals:

The Kingdom Voice, **Rev. Reginald Bradbury, publisher and editor;** *News of the World; Sunday Express; The Sunday Times; New Life Magazine; Viewpoint Aquarius; Southern I.T.V.* **(all in England), and reporter and spokesman Ivor Hills, Radio London; Rex Dutta, reporter.**

Here is the full and most complete documented story of what has come to be called the "VOICE FROM SPACE." The "Voice from Outer Space" broke into the scheduled news bulletin being read by Ivor Mills on Southern I.T.V. at 5:12 PM on November 26, 1977, overriding the TV signal and broadcasting its own message for five and one-half minutes.

The authorities fell over themselves in their haste to denounce it as a fake, but let us consider this more carefully. It could not be hushed-up or ignored as so many flying saucer events deliberately are, because hundreds of thousands of TV viewers heard this broadcast. It was heard as far apart as Winchester, Andover, Newbury, Reading, London, Southampton, Oxford and elsewhere - doubtless the number of listeners ran into the millions. Listeners were impressed both by the strong voice and by its content. Most were greatly moved; a faction was shocked and apprehensive. The press played up this minority, never once reporting the majority, who were deeply touched and were helped by the space offer of friendship and encouragement, albeit with a **warning of the need for us to change.**

A strange truth was found in that *nobody reported the message in full!* Though only five and one-half minutes long, it was never broadcast in its entirety - only the first thirty seconds. And always this same segment, which did not give a balanced view. NO newspaper gave the full transcript. Why? Did the authorities fear the full hearing/reading by the public? Why the rush to decry it as a hoax?

Typical News Accounts Given

News of the World (England), Nov. 27, 1988: (ITV): A southern ITV spokesman said later, "We have been flooded with calls. Our engineers are trying to discover exactly what happened. We're assuming it was rather a sick hoax. We can't imagine how it was done, but it appears that someone must have managed to transmit a signal over ours. The equipment used would need to be fairly sophisticated and expensive."

The Sun (England), Nov. 28, 1977: "Post Office experts tracked down the hoax transmission to Hannington, Herts. But they still do not know who was responsible or how it was done."

Sunda Express (England), Nov. 27, 1977: "A post office spokesman said either a transmitter or some kind of link into land lines was used by someone, and they managed to get access to the transmitters at Rowridge and Bennington."

At least two transmitters were taken over. The *Sunday Times*, Dec. 4, 1977, a full week later, was being used by the authorities to push the "official explanation" that students using just 80 pounds ($) worth of equipment, powered by an ordinary car battery, sneaked up to the base of the Bennington mast and beamed in the pirate signal. But how about the mast at Rowridge many miles away? How was that simultaneously overridden? And wasn't it also true that *more* than two masts were overridden simultaneously? Were not *five points* used to cut in? This has *not been published at all.* The *Sunday Times* went on to give the explanation of students in a van doing the pirating. "Pirates" would also have to beat the I.B.A.'s monitoring system. Engineers at centers around Britain watch for "faults" in transmission and can switch off sections of the network.

Engineers at Croydon, supposedly monitoring Bennington's transmission, failed to log the galactic message. In fact, the engineers at Croyden *did not even hear the message!* They were unaware that the space broadcast was overriding their own signal! Simultaneously, the main TV transmitter at Southampton also did not know it was being overridden, nor did its monitoring system record the space voice!

Nothing untoward was showing on the electrical dials or instruments, because the *Space Voice* was not using earth electricity. By law, all radio and TV stations have a monitoring system for instant switch-off should revolutionaries break in or some speaker blaspheme. The 150 booster masts are unguarded physically, but all are equipped with safeguards, like coded messages - technically known as insertion test signals which the viewer does not see or hear. As the *Sunday Times* stated, there exists a round-the-clock surveillance system. It all failed. It did not even register space interruption, which was *not using earth electricity.*

Earth Electricity was Not Used

According to an opinion voiced by the *Viewpoint Aquarius*, the "space voice" used some form of occult powers. That is why nothing registered on the TV monitor's dials, and why the main TV monitor did not make a tape of the message. The engineers did not even know their station had been taken over, and were therefore *powerless* to cut off the broadcast. It is for these reasons that the authorities were, or are, so worried and prefer you to believe it was all a hoax!

It is my opinion that the power used was something else, and has more to do with *Tensor Calculations* and the

110

Quantums of Light-Beam Transmission Wave Frequencies, especially in the form of "communication via UFOs" to planets and persons.

Again, we quote from the *Viewpoint Aquarius*: "In December, 1975, when a flying saucer came right down over Horris Green in Liverpool, dozens of space images materialized in the living rooms of the surrounding houses; hundreds of local TV sets showed the space images. (Authors note: Some TV sets were *not* even turned on!) Thousands of residents came out of their homes to stare at the saucer. When a 'voice from outer space' phoned into Radio London in January, 1971, while Rex Dutta was actually broadcasting, the engineers were flabbergasted because there was no echo or feedback, i.e., *nothing was registering on the dials in their transmitting stations, although the 'space voice' was being clearly heard by all in the studio.* Normally, the needles on the dials rise and fall as a human voice is loud or soft, and the electrical pulses register on the instruments. In this case, the needles were inert at zero. The 'voice' was clear. No earthling instrument was used. But unknown power was ...." (The rest of the report is too lengthy to be included).

Viewpoint Aquarius had tried three major networks using quite high level inside contacts, but kept getting fobbed off with the same 30 second segment that had already been broadcast. So too did other researchers and the *National Press*. There was just no full record of the total five and one-half minutes. Quoting again from Viewpoint Aquarius:

"This effective cover-up was broken by only one magazine and we are happy to pay tribute to it - *THE NEW LIFE MAGAZINE*, London, England. Once we knew the full tape existed, in spite of ITV denials, we too, eventually and with great perseverance, actually heard it, thanks to the courtesy of the senior officials at London Broadcasting Company."

"After playing the tape repeatedly through very sophisticated studio equipment, we are confident *(Viewpoint*

Aquarius version) it is a definite rendering of the rather difficult to decipher 'voice' sounding deep as though coming through water (heavy, slow and wavering, as if it were more mechanical than one of manned-type agency). There is only one single point of doubt - that is the name of the 'voice'. The press has given this variously as *Trillion, Gillon, Glon.* We *(Viewpoint Aquarius)* are sufficiently rash as to state, after listening on really top equipment at deliberately varied speeds, the name is *Gramaha* or *Bramaha.*" (Authors note: It could also be *Gamaah* or *Bamaah,* the spelling being phonetic).

Message From Space on Southern TV

Following is the reprinted version of the event from *New Life Magazine,* as it was sent from the now defunct *Xenolog* newsletter in New Zealand by Rev. Reginald Bradbury of the *Kingdom Voice.* We quote from the edition of *Xenolog,* Winter, No. 116, September 4, 1978. Extract from *New Life Magazine,* London, England.

"After going to press, we managed to obtain the hitherto unpublished complete transcript of the 'voice' intervention 'from outer space' that occurred on Southern Television in the Bennington area at 5:05 PM on Saturday, November 26, 1977, and we thought it was of sufficient interest to warrant this report."

"It was widely reported in the National Press in the next days that the deep echoing 'voice' and its unearthly 'message' were threatening and had generated widespread fear among viewers. No newspaper quoted the message accurately or attempted to precisely report the theme of it, for no complete recording was available. Southern Television only records their broadcasts from their main transmitter, not from each relay station, and few viewers were sufficiently equipped and alert enough to tape more than just the last few words of the five and one-half minute interruption. Consequently, journalists were only able to report the recollections of viewers, and it is likely that it was the most alarmed ones that contacted the police or press. It is hardly surprising, therefore, that the impression given by the press was misleading. Furthermore, the first thirty seconds of the message has been broadcast several times by L.B.C. on their news programs, but on each occasion the calming second sentence was edited out, thereby subtly distorting the balance of the message. The focus of these broadcasts lay upon the eerie sound of the 'voice,' but the content of the message was neither referred to nor discussed. We are publishing it here in full to get the record straight, and because we think the message has merit, regardless of origin." (NOTE: Brackets ( ) used to include a difference in the "message" quote).

The Message

Following is the message heard over the ITV station:

This is the Voice of Gamaah (Gramaha), the Representative of the ASTERON (Ashtar) GALACTIC COMMAND, speaking to you. For many years you have seen us as lights in the sky. We speak to you now in peace and wisdom, as we have done to your brothers and sisters all over this, your planet Earth. We come to warn you of the destiny of your race and your world, so that you may communicate to your fellow beings the course you must take to avoid the disaster which threatens your world and the beings on the other worlds around you. This is in order that you may share in the great awakening as the planet passes into the New Age of Aquarius. The New Age can be a time of great evolution for your race, but only if your rulers are made aware of the evil forces that can overshadow their judgment.

Be still now and listen! For your chance may not come again for many years. Your scientists, governments and generals have not heeded our warnings. They have continued to experiment with the evil forces of what you call nuclear energy. Atomic bombs can destroy the earth and the beings of your sister worlds in a moment. The wastes from atom power systems will poison your planet for many thousands of your years to come. We who have followed the path of evolution for far longer than you have long since realized this - that atomic energy is always directed <u>against</u> life. It has no peaceful application. Its use, and research into use, must be ceased at once or you will risk destruction. All weapons of evil must be removed. The time of conflict is now past and the races of which you are a part may proceed to the highest planes of evolution if you show yourselves worthy to do this. You have but a short time to learn to live together in peace and goodwill. Small groups all over the planet are learning this and exist to pass on the light of the dawning New Age to you all. You are free to accept or reject their teaching, but only those who learn to live in peace will pass to the higher realms of spiritual evolution.

Hear now the Voice of GAMAAH (Gramaha), the Voice of the ASTERON (Ashtar) GALACTIC COMMAND speaking to you. Be aware also that there are many false prophets and guides at present operating on your world. They will suck your energy from you - the energy you call money - and will put it to evil ends giving you worthless dross in return. Your Inner Self will protect you from this. You must learn to be sensitive to the Voice from within that can tell you what is confusion, chaos and untruth. Learn to be sensitive to the Voice of Truth which is within you, and you will lead yourselves onto the path of evolution.

This is our message to you, our dear friends. We have watched you growing for many years, as you too have watched our lights in your skies. You know now that we are here, and that there are more beings on and around your earth than your scientists admit. We are deeply concerned about you and your path toward the light, and will do all we can to help you. Have no fears. Seek only to know yourselves and live in harmony with the way of your planet Earth. We of the ASTERON (Ashtar) GALACTIC COMMAND thank you for your attention. We are now leaving the planes of your existence. May you be blessed by the supreme love and truth of the Cosmos.

In his book *Prelude to the Landing on Planet Earth,* which was previewed in the last issue of *Xenolog* (Summer Issue, No. 115), Stuart Holroyd stated that the plan to interrupt television and radio transmission during the period of November 18 - 22, 1977 was still on – "It may not be with the fullest force, but it will be their beginning. Also, it might afford an opportunity to alert the people of the world to what their governments had in mind." This is a remarkably prophetic statement if one considers the timing. My own *source* informed me in the early 1960's that the people of space would make use of our communicating and space satellite TV media to speak to those of earth and to show images of *their* ships or *beings.* We have been reliably informed that this has happened more frequently than has

115

been reported by press, radio or TV media. Instead, it has been suppressed. Of course, there are those who will claim that the hoaxers had read the book, or at least knew of the experience it described. That might be so, but would that also explain the release in November 1977 of Steven Spielberg's spectacular UFO film, *Close Encounter of the Third Kind* that postulates a mass landing of UFOs on earth? The film was the subject of the cover story of *Newsweek* of November 21, 1977, under the headline *THE UFOs ARE COMING*. Its title alone, *Prelude to the Landing on Planet Earth,* could be seen to anticipate a similar event. Furthermore, the source of the communications analyzed therein reaffirmed the point in the following message:

> *We speak to the people of planet earth. It is of great importance that you have the understanding that we come only in love and peace. It is a time of importance in the universe that the planet Earth be evolved and the consciousness of those that exist upon the planet be raised to a higher degree. It is also important for you to understand that we cannot permit, in the present or in the future, any more devastation upon earth. There are those civilizations that are in service in the universe that are in motion to come to your earth, not only to give mankind the benefit of their medical and technological skills, but also their love. They are in service to the planet earth and to the universe. We conveyed to Sir John (Whitemore) and to the doctor (Puharich), that we would interfere on your radio and television communication systems to relay when the civilizations are coming close to landing on your planet.*
>
> *It is now in motion. We wish you to know that we love you. We wish for there not*

to be panic on earth, for we come in peace,
but it is also important for the people of earth
to recognize that the civilizations that come -
come in brotherhood to help them. It is
important now to become one with the broth-
erhood of the Universe. We ask that those on
earth do not attempt to prevent the
civilizations that are coming, but to accept
them in love, even though the earth has
caused devastation to itself, and in turn,
contaminated the universe. We are with you;
we love you and we come in peace.

Whatever we think of the above statement, it nonetheless should give us pause to think about the peril of the time in which we live, and about what action we feel necessary within the legal framework of our own nation to prevent more destruction and violence from occurring. Are we willing to open the way for the *coming of our brothers from space* at long last?

CHAPTER TEN
PROPHECIES NOW UNDERSTOOD

Let those who come for the words they shall hear;
Draw close, draw close, open your ear.
Prophets are speaking, 'tis words of the future that ring clear;
Draw close, draw close, open your ear.
Shall our future be void of fear?
Shall our future be bright and clear?
Prophets are speaking, 'tis words of the future that ring clear;
What say you prophets; what say you all?
How shall the future unfold for us now?
Draw close, draw close, open your ear;
For words of the ancients and prophets ring clear.

The following is a selection of prophecies relating to the present time period in which we find ourselves. These prophecies, many of which are some 3,000 years old in origin, are now fitting together as long lost parts of an enigmatic puzzle. It is hoped that they will help to more clearly elucidate our alternatives in this "Time of Tribulations: Period II: Era of Desolation."

Messages from the Virgin Mary

We owe credit and source for the following information by the former *"Axminster Light Centre"* in England:

"The appearance of Mary, mother of Jesus, has been occasioned by significant phenomena wherever she has made an appearance (Guadeloupe, Mexico 1531; La Salette, France 1846; Fatima, Portugal 1917; Germany May, 1946; Garabandal, Spain, 1961-1965; and Zeitoun, Egypt, 1963-1965). Many have been witness to the appearances of doves and angels; even the sun seeming to spin in the sky and coming down so as to light up a large area. But of all the alleged phenomena, our attention should be directed to the prophecies that have been given in the form of messages and warnings, as those that follow:"

If my people will not submit, I shall be forced to let go of my Son's arm. It is so strong and heavy that I can no longer hold it up. And with your prayers and works you can never make up for all the trouble I have taken on your behalf. If the harvest is ruined, it is your fault. Pass on my message to my people. (Message given to Melanie Calvert of La Salette, France in 1846).

The children of Fatima, Portugal received the following message in the year 1917:

The Lord is offended. Pray for the conversion of your country. Above all, accept and bear with submission for the sufferings and the Universal Immutable Law that God will send you. Pray for sinners ... pray for the sick world.

On November 26, 1957, Lucy, who was the sole survivor of the three children of Fatima, stated:
"Three times Our Lady has told me we are approaching the Latter Days. We still have time to check heaven's punishment by prayer and repentance for our mistakes, both as individuals and as a race on earth."

Mary gave a message to Lucy which is *not* in the Pope's apartments in the Vatican. Only part of this message has been revealed to the public:

Proclaim in My Name: A punishment will befall the entire human race. It will not come today or tomorrow, but in the second half of the Twentieth Century ... the human race has sinned and trampled with its feet the gift that

119

was bestowed on it. Nowhere does order reign.

Satan (sin or error) has reached the very highest place and decides the march of events. He will succeed in introducing himself into and reaching the highest summit of the Church. He will succeed in seducing the minds of great scholars who will invent weapons with which it will be possible to destroy half of mankind in a matter of minutes. He will have powerful nations under his empire, and he will lead them in the mass production of these weapons. If mankind does not take steps to stop him, I shall be obliged to let my Son's arm fall (the sword of Truth), (Authors note: Hindus Satya Yuga; Age of Truth), and then God will punish men far more severely than when He did so by means of the flood.

The great and powerful will perish in the same way as the weak and small. But a time of severe trials will also come to the Church. Cardinal will oppose Cardinal, and Bishop will oppose Bishop. Fire and smoke will then fall from the heavens, and the waters of the oceans will boil—then evaporate. The spray will leap into the sky and everything that is standing will sink. Millions of men will perish by the hour, and those who are left alive will envy those who have died.

In Germany after the end of World War II, this message was given to Ms. Barbara Ruess:

I cannot manifest My power to the world in general, upon you it depends to shorten the days of darkness. This is My message to the world, and all people must be informed about it ... A NEW REVELATION has been made to the world and they will experience what has been revealed.

In January, 1965, Conchita, one of the four children who were witnesses to the appearance of Our Lady of Garabandal, Spain, received the following message which was to be communicated to the world:

As my message of October 18th (the third message which was given earlier at Fatima, Portugal in 1917) has not been complied with, and it has not been communicated to the world, I am telling you that this is the LAST ONE I SHALL GIVE. Previously the Cup was filling up, now it is brimming over. Many are following the road to Perdition, and with them they are taking many souls. We should turn the wrath of God (i.e., taking on personal responsibility). If you ask His forgiveness with a sincere heart, He will pardon you!

Conchita relates: The Virgin told me that it (the secret she is not permitted to speak of) will be visible to everybody, everywhere! It will be a direct work of God, and will take place before the Great Miracle. I do not know whether people will die because of it. They could only die from the shock of seeing it ... (the interpretation here is that *two events* are to happen; one is a sign to alert mankind to mend their ways, and the other is a miracle - something that will happen that will affect all of us).

Conchita went on to say, "It will be a *direct work of God,* and in the order of a phenomenon similar to *fire or light.* (Authors note: Possible aerobolide?) It will be seen first in the sky. It will be seen by all. Then it will be present everywhere, and will be felt by all, no matter where one would be at the time. It will be as if our sins will be revealed to us. I do not know how long it will last, but *within ten minutes after its start, the entire world will be in terror!* Mary told only me about the *miracle.* She forbade me to say what it will consist of. I cannot reveal the date until eight days beforehand, but it will be half-past eight on a Thursday evening."

She then describes a scene that will be visible to everyone in her village and on the surrounding mountainside. The sick who will be present will be *cured* and the doubting ones will *believe,* and it will be the greatest miracle that Jesus has ever worked in the world!

Conchita continues, "There will not remain the slightest doubt that *it comes from God and is for the good of Mankind.* In the pine grove at Garabandal a sign of the Miracle will be left at that spot forever as proof. It will be possible to film and televise the whole thing, but the *Sign* cannot be touched. It will be recognized as a *thing not of this world,* and that it comes from God."

In addressing herself to the coming *punishment,* Conchita says, "If the punishment does take place, then I know what it will consist of because Mary told me. What is more, I have seen it...."

The Indian Brothers Speak

One of our good Indian brothers and an honored prophet among the Hopi Nation, Mr. Thomas Banyacya (now deceased), once made this statement about the times to come: "You will know the time is near when the *tops of the trees begin to wither and die* (smog and pollution). You will know the time is very near when *men go to another world and bring back minerals to this world* (trips to our moon by the Apollo Astronauts of the USA Space program). The *light will come at breakfast,* and you will only have time to walk to your door, open it and WATCH!"

Mr. Banyacya, together with other honored Indian prophets, such as Mr. David Monongwe, Andrew Hermesquaftewa, Oswald "White Bear" Fredericks, and Chief Daniel Katchongva have added, "You will know the time when all these things come to pass when *men shall build a house in the sky and go and live in it!*" (NASA's Space Shuttle Program and the construction of a space station between the earth and the moon. Perhaps it will be finished in the future, barring any great conflict in the world).

The Hopi have had a traditional belief that if the white brothers Bahanna do not return to their *true teachings* given to them by the *same great world teacher*, the Messiah, whom they speak of as *Massau'u* through the Great Spirit Taiowa, then the world will again be destroyed, or at least millions of people killed! They also state that unless the white man allows the Hopi to keep their land (there has been a somewhat *secret plan* for the Indian nations to sell off their reservations and to live as do their white brothers, which would bring about the demise of the Indian peoples), the Savior Massau'u as *Pahanna - the True Brother*, could not return to them as promised. Instead, another race, the Ant people, or those who live in closely-knit and highly ordered and regulated societies (authors note: possibly from the Far East, who number in millions) will come to the far West, bringing great *population or armies*. Our civilization, as we have known it, could be DESTROYED!

* * * * * * *

"When a gourd of molten ashes (atomic bomb) [20]
Falls to earth from out of heaven,
When all roads lead to Oraibi,
And the Spider's web is made (highways)

When the Hopi journeys Eastward
To the House of Mica or glass (UN building) [21]

---

[20] They shall make a little ball that will fall to the earth, and the earth will be devastated...A gourd of molten ashes falls from out of heaven."

Listen, Listen, White Man, Brother.
For the Day is close upon us,
Will the Great Massau'u return,
Or will there come the Terrible One?

But if the Sacred Land is taken,
Then comes the changing of the Seasons,
Earth will quake, and from the West wind,
There will come the Terrible One.

If he comes, with population,
Planes and guns surround the nation,
And all transportation ceases,
Days of horror .... Terrible One!

And as in the world before us,
World so long ago forgotten,
Earth did quake, and the great mountains
Split and fell into the sea (Atlantis).

So this day is close upon us.
When our Earth will shake and tremble,
And as Old World, soon forgotten,
So our land will no more be.

---

[21] The Hopi Indian prophets traveled to the UN building many years ago
and because their 'credentials' were improper by the UN's standards (i.e.,
no proper admittance identification pass into the General Assembly, but
only the 'Sacred Bundle' given through direction of the Great Spirit
Father), they were turned away and unable to carry their message of
warning to all of the nations gathered there at that time. The Hopi
prophets had been told that this would not be surprising because it was
further prophesied on their Sacred Stone Tablet: "For that which had not
been told them they SHALL SEE, and for that which they DID NOT
HEAR, they WOULD CONSIDER." Chief Dan Katchongva said,
"Many people living at that time will live to see the White Brother
(Pahanna) return to the earth, and when they do they will live to consider
what they could have heard if they had permitted the original inhabitants
of this, the Americas, to give a message to that great body of people."

Listen, listen, White Man, Brother,
For that Day is close upon us,
Day of Purification comes
And Day of Hopi prophesies."

The following information also comes from the Hopi prophecies:

A series of earthquakes would be felt throughout this land (USA) and would come as warnings to the people to repent. If they do not heed the warnings of people and repent before it is too late, a bad earthquake will strike, devastating many cities and resulting in the death of large masses. Floods would be seen in places where they have never been seen before. There would be a great climatic changes world-wide. Where it is hot, it becomes cold; where it was dry is now wet. In each case it would be the worst recorded in history. (Authors note: Magnetic polar shift?)

There would be famine, pestilence, disease and plague throughout the land. The Hopi were warned never to depend upon great inventions that would be brought to them by the coming white race. They were told by the White Brother that a lighting system would be established throughout this land, and all one had to do was touch the wall to light the room. However, if they depended on that light, they would be sorry because it would be cut off at once and the people left in panic. They wouldn't know how to get along without it. They were told to depend on the old ways and they would always survive. They were also warned against running water that would come into their homes. This water would be polluted and anyone depending upon it would die or get terribly sick.

There would be terrible fighting all over the land. City against city, village against village, and family against family. The whole continent would be in disorder. The Hopi were warned to stay on their reservation, and they would be able to avoid this trouble. They could go on living the same way as they had done for centuries past. The Hopi do not want a lot of people to rush there thinking they will be protected, because they only have enough for their own people. Those who have been warned and do not obey the warning would possibly be destroyed before they could get there.

The moon will turn to blood, and the sun will hide its face. The seasons will change, and ice will flow from the north countries.

The Great Ones Come: Day of Purification
by Chief Dan Kachongva

It is known to all TRUE BROTHERS and to all INDIAN BROTHERS who have returned to the simple ways of the reservation, or those who have returned to the more natural ways of the Great Spirit or the Lord God, Father of Lights, that "... when the TRUE WHITE BROTHER returns HE will be all-powerful and will wear a RED CAP or RED CLOAK. He will be large in population, belong to no religion but His own. He will bring with Him the Sacred Stone Tablets. Great will be His coming. None will be able to stand against Him. All power in this world will be placed in His hand, and He will come swiftly, and in one day get control of this whole continent. Hopi has been warned never to take up arms."

With Him there will be TWO GREAT ONES, both very intelligent and powerful, one of whom will have a symbol or sign of SWASTIKA which represents PURITY, and is a male. The second or third of the two helpers of True White Brotherhood will have a sign of a symbol of the SUN. He, too, will be many people, very intelligent and powerful. (Authors note: Dalai Lama and his assistants who visited the Hopi!)

This, the Hopi say, represents the world, and that when the time of *Purification Day* is near, those with these signs, SWASTIKA and SUN, will SHAKE THE EARTH FIRST FOR A SHORT PERIOD OF TIME in preparation for the final Day of Purification. They will shake the earth two times (Germany and Japan?), then will come as one to

126

bring on Purification Day, and to help his younger Brother who waits in this land.

It is also prophesied that if these three fail to carry out their mission, then the One from the West will come like a TERRIBLE STORM. He will be many, many people and an unmerciful one. When he comes he will cover the land like ants. The Hopi people have been warned not to get up on their rooftops to watch, as he will come to punish all the people. They do not know who this man is, only that he will have a *large* population. If none of these fulfill their mission, the Hopi leaders will place their prayer feathers to the Four Corners of the Hearth and appeal to the Great Spirit, and He will cause a force of Light to strike the earth people. Only those with the spirit of righteousness will survive. However, if all people turn away from the great spirit, He will cause the earth to be destroyed once again. We of the human race shall have lost the chance to enter Everlasting Life. They say the ANTS (race of large population) may inhabit the Earth after that.

But if these three carry out and fulfill their mission, and if one, two or three Hopi remain steadfast to their Ancient Teaching or Instructions, (making no war and not allowing oil or uranium on their land to be used for warlike purposes, which is still being contested with the U. S. Government) then the Great Spirit, Massau'u as Pahanna, will appear before all that are saved and the THREE will lay out a NEW LIFE PLAN which leads to Everlasting Life. This Earth will be renewed, as it was from the beginning. Flowers will bloom again, wild game will return, and there will be an abundance of food for all. Those who are saved will share everything equally, and they will all recognize the Great Spirit. They may intermarry and speak one tongue. A new religion or spiritual understanding will be set up if the people desire it.

Cleansing Cycle

We have talked of the *Coming Changes,* as seen by many of the Hopi Indian Nation. We shall continue this line of information as to the *Cleansing Cycle* upon which we have entered here on the earth, and the changes which this will bring us. Let us start with a prophecy of the *Jicarilla Apache Indian.*

"Then the Jacarilla Apache came from the underworld. They didn't know what had happened before this. The people came up and traveled all around the world. Dios (God) told these eight people who could travel with their eyes, 'Now you had better go back in the mountains.' These eight were separate from the twenty-four in the other mountains. These eight were among the Apache for awhile. They told the Apaches of what had happened before. That is why the Apache know this story. Four of the eight went to Wide Grass, a mountain. It is near Antonito, south of Antonito. Red Mountain was the other mountain. It is near the Rio Grande, south of Wide Grass Mountain. Four went in there. Dios told them, 'You must come back when the earth is destroyed again.'"

"At the end of the world these people who travel with their eyes are going to come back and go to all directions and see what is happening in the East, South, West and North. For the telephone and telegraph are not going to be here anymore. They are all going to burn. *Next time the earth will be destroyed by fire.* All are going to be destroyed. Maybe another world will be made, I don't know."

128

"At Taos (New Mexico) where there used to be a lake (see *Blue Lake*), there is now some soft ground. There have been two fires there. When four fires have occurred there, the earth is going to be destroyed. The first time that there was a fire at that place the Pueblos went and dug a ditch to it and tried to put it out with water, but the water burned like oil. Finally, they called upon an old Apache man and woman. The man's name was *Banan*; the woman's name I do not know. They don't say how these two put out the fire, but they did put it out."

"The second time it burned, I was alive. I saw it from a distance. An old Apache who had just died awhile back stopped the fire. It will burn twice more. The fourth time no one will be able to stop it. The fire is going to start there and burn all over the world."

The Fire Cycle

The early Mayans of Yucatan, as well as the various nations of Indian peoples who inhabited what is now called Mexico, also had prophesies which spoke of this era of our time cycles as the FIFTH CYCLE. It was their belief, along with many of the North American Indians, that our present world civilization would be purified by *fire*. However, this would be preceded by *world floods* in which many cities and people would be lost. There is a further Indian prophecy which has to do with the location of the present Indian nations which stated, "Three times shall the Red Man travel the earth, and then he shall stop and begin to build his home, and then shall the White Man begin his travels." (This is all too true in our present time!)

Papal Prophecies

Under a NEW POPE (De Gloria Olivae: *From the Glory of the Olive*) in the year 1998, there will be many startling changes which have already begun under the pope who was so very popular for such a short time period. This pope's *true* title should have been POPE PIUS XII (claimed by the earlier Pope Eugenio Pacelli, the last of the Popes under the "Consolation Period") - PASTORE ANGELICUS. His title was given by the early Irish seer and Holy Prophet, St. Malachy: *De Mediaete Lunae - Of the Middle of the Moon.*

Pope John Paul I reigned exactly 26 days after confirmation, and then expired. On September 13th, in the middle of his Pontificate, there appeared a *full moon*. Therefore, one might say that his was also a *half moon*! Again referring to St Malachy: "From the *half-moon* proceeds this Pope sent to Rome by the Divine doctor. Hail, oh, our well beloved Father, Pius XII, most Holy Mediator, future victim."

Pope John Paul's papal birth symbol was CANCER - the CRAB. It was the beginning of much breakdown and breaking away from very strict edicts within the structure of the Holy Mother Church. There was also great persecution from the areas of the Middle East and African nations, who by reason of their Mohammedan Faith are under the symbol of the CATIF of the MOON (Crescent moon). This had been identified by John of Revelations as DHUL QUARNAIN - the two-horned winged dragon. This persecution shall continue under the present Pope John Paul II or "DE LABORE SUIS" (Sun) and become more severe under the new Pope, as pagans will join in bringing about persecution, disruption, and great damage to churches and spiritual works. Then there shall also be great strides in spiritual understanding to accept this final period of *atonement, resurrection in spirit, and grace of the Christus.* This is a lull period between that of the "Consolation" and the "Desolation" periods which shall finally consummate itself in the frenzied final battle of "Dark and Light Forces" referred to as ARMAGEDDON, if changes are not brought about.

I was also given the following prophetical quatrain from my own extraterrestrial *source*:

"Upon the Throne of Peter, a NEW POPE to be, and with change misfortune, new woes to see. Ruin, pillage, death, ravaged Italy. For though his motto be: 'To contemplate the Moon, his gaze will find bloody scenes, as MOORS again sound their fervored tune.'"

The prophecy concludes with the quatrain:

"When this drama doth draw near, the decade shall have passed a YEAR. Many have cause to fear, for DAY has passed; NIGHT IS HERE!"

During this period there would also be certain *other signs*, such as Sacred Laws as well as Christianity becoming eclipsed by other more selfish laws. Gold and silver will have found a new owner, being bought and sold both in the open and black market, dealing for what it can bring rather than as it had once been as legal backing and industrial application. A changing of doctrines and attacks by more materialistic attitude and unchanging philosophies, sacred laws go largely unheeded and unobserved. Thus, why Christianity is disturbed greatly about *peace, law and order*. Greed, avarice, covetedness, gluttony, lust, and slovenliness are now patterns which are commonly seen and accepted as the rule rather than the exception. This shall finally lead the world to the brink of a world-wide catastrophe, as it will be the "warning flag" prior to both a war of unprecedented nature, and at the same time period, an upheaval of nature on a scale never before in our time seen or known by mankind!

It appears that nature itself, violated by man, will rebel. There will be cataclysms of many types - floods, atmospheric disturbance with resulting destruction, added to which shall be pestilence and famine. The awakening countries will disappear and actual distribution of oceans will be changed by successive waves of disasters on a cataclysmic scale. The northern Balkans—Northern Holland, Denmark, Northern Germany, Northern Poland and Northwestern Russia—for instance, can conceivably become covered by seas, which would include the former nations of Lithuania, Latvia, and Estonia. It will find Southern France, as well as Southern Spain and a great part of the Italian Peninsula also covered by the waters of the Western Mediterranean. In the Orient, the nation of Japan, as well as the Kurile Islands and parts of China and Southeast Asia will suffer. The former will have complete submersion; the latter, partial submersion!

Dr. Milton A. Nobles, geologist and a student of earthquakes and volcanic activity, predicts a second deluge during which *whole continents will be obliterated and new ones created.* He sees new lands rising to double the area of the western hemisphere, and states that Australia and New Zealand will join in a continent *three times their present size!* He prophesies the *shortening of the earth's axis* with a new North Pole in Siberia, and a new South Pole in the South Pacific Ocean. He states that there will be a new equator with the United States so close that the all-year mildness of Florida will be the whole nation's temperature. New sea coasts in the Atlantic and Pacific will arise. The Gulf of Mexico will be transformed into an inland sea the size of Texas, and Central America and the West Indies amalgamated in the new America, 5,000 miles wide!

"And then shall they see the Son of Man coming in the clouds with great power and glory. And then shall He send His angels, and shall gather together His Elect from the four winds, from the uttermost part of the earth to the uttermost part of heaven." (Mark 13:26-27). Regarding the coming of the angels with the Christ, most of the Aquarian

Age prophets and many of the older prophets interpreted this as significant of the *arrival physically of the spiritual manifestation of the great Light of Christ.* These beings who have evolved far beyond our present life pattern represent a high spiritual quality so that they can be of aid in helping to elevate the spiritual level of earth and the consciousness of mankind.

> "Oh, humanity, will you work to cut thyself off from pain and to prevent anyone else from feeling ill? Feel once more He who is in the world until its ending. It will not be a cross with nails, but a Solar Cross shining in thee, radiating your life all round, a Solar Cross which announces coming events to the world. The Eternal will come to help you. You know how to understand His reappearance."

Nuclear Hazard Areas

Our *sources* have stated that in times to come nuclear hazard areas will be sealed for at least ten to fifteen years due to their complete disruption and "melt-down."

Some of these nuclear hazard areas will be found in *Mexico City*, a region just to the north of *Ciudad, Mexico* or *Districto Federales de Ciudad, Mexico;* in the southeastern areas of *Louisiana, Tennessee, New Jersey, and New York,* and in the states of *Wisconsin, Minnesota, Kansas, Idaho, Nevada, Washington, California, and Arizona.*

There will also be nuclear hazard areas in the nations of *Israel, Pakistan, India, Japan (Nippon), People's Republic of China, the Commonwealth of Independent States, and the Commonwealth of the Dominion of Canada.*

These are, in the main, areas that will be "SEALED" due to high levels of radiation. These areas will be a danger to life that remains as a *Remnant* upon the planet following the *Cleansing Period.*

133

CHAPTER ELEVEN
REVELATIONS

Is there a relationship between the UFOs and parallel worlds existing in a different time-zone dimension; the imminent return of Jesus, and also certain dramatic events which are taking place here and now—events which are closely linked with the prophecies of both Old and New Testaments concerning the last days of Planet Earth in this Age?

John The Divine

It was to commune with God that the great seer, St. John the Divine, sought solitude on the lonely and beautiful island of Patmos. Yet he could never have foreseen the stupendous nature of the vision about to be revealed to him. During his solitary vigil he was, as he says, "in the Spirit." That is, his soul had temporarily vacated his physical body to enter those dimensions which we call the *etheric* or *spiritual*. There the concepts of time and space have no meaning. In this state of heightened awareness John was able to observe the material universe, as well as the *etheric-spiritual* universe simultaneously, and to see the past, present and future in one.

In the very first chapter of the Book of Revelations we read how John witnessed the triumphant arrival of the Christus and His Angelic Host in their interdimensional craft, described here as "clouds," and elsewhere in the Scriptures as "chariots" or "whirlwinds." The Master's arrival is witnessed not only by John, but by all the inhabitants of the etheric (parallel worlds or dimensions) including his own executioners trapped in the lower astral regions. John immediately prostrates himself before the Christ who commands him to write down all that he is about to see. "Behold, I shall come quickly," He warns again, referring to His second return to earth. "Hold fast to that (scriptural knowledge) which you have, so that no man shall

134

take your crown (of enlightenment and peace), for he who overcomes (earthly temptations and trials) I will make a pillar in the Temple of my God, and he shall no more go out." (Rev. 3:12). There will be no more earthly incarnations for those who are true to His teachings!

An interesting physical description of the Christus is given in (Rev. 2:13-16), suggesting that in His own parallel world dimension, His natural appearance is very different from that of earthlings. The description tallies with those of space entities given in the Old Testament books of Daniel, Ezekiel and elsewhere, and again, (Rev. 1:17-18) tells us that John was frightened until the Master identified Himself.

After this, he tells us, "A door was opened in heaven," and a voice said, "Come up here and I will show you the things which will be hereafter." John found himself in the presence of a majestic Being (angelic description), who is seated upon a throne and surrounded by a rainbow of emerald-colored light (President of the solar system, Salon Three?). This wonderful Being is surrounded by twenty-four attendants, or Elders clothed in white and wearing what appears to be Golden Helmets on their heads (authors note: These could be the twelve Counselor-Masters and the twelve Elder-Masters representing the "powers" of our Solar Government). Other attendant creatures described as some type of "beasts with eyes" are also present. (authors note: possible androids or robotic creatures with "constructed intelligence" who can compute derived information from whatever source and report on their findings). Again, the overall description is of some type of spacecraft (authors note: Sea of burning glass or manufactured crystal-matrix) upon which is found highly intelligent life together with its commander and crew. The "thunderings and lightenings" emanating from it (sounds and force field) tallies with that given also in the Book of Ezekial, Chapter 1, and elsewhere.

It is probable that this mighty *Being* referred to throughout the Scriptures as "the Lord" is the Supreme Commander of our galaxy (Ophuchius-Serpent Holder). The entities referred to throughout the Bible as "angels" are most

135

probably space beings, and would be His own subjects and messengers. There appears to be overwhelming evidence biblically for this, and for the statements contained in the following paragraphs. It should be firmly borne in mind that nowhere in either the Old or New Testament does the Lord, or His son, Jesus the Christus, claim to be the Supreme Being; that infinite, formless, unknowable First Cause of the entire Universe, even though for thousands of years theologians have made claims to the opposite.

We do not dispute such a claim that He is indeed the creator of humankind, our immediate galaxy, and all the chemical life-forms therein. We have no reason to disbelieve this claim. It is probable that the parallel world dimension peoples have existed for eons longer than ourselves, and may have perfected techniques of genetic engineering, suspended animation and bionics so advanced that our limited imagination cannot conceive of this type of science. If so, this could help to explain some of the prolonged life-spans of the ancient patriarchs of the Old Testament, such as Methuselah, who appeared to be in constant contact with space beings (angels of the Lord, or simply the Host) and lived for hundreds of years.

Nevertheless, the Lord, our Creator, never denies that He, Himself, could be the product of an even higher creative intelligence, or that He, like ourselves, is animated by the Holy Spirit to which He, like us, is ultimately answerable! It has been stated and shown in spiritual teachings that the Father, Son and Holy Spirit are three aspects of one Supreme Being as taught by theologians throughout the ages. That they are in fact three *separate* entities, the latter being superior to the former two, was openly stated by the Christus Himself when He warns that although blasphemy against the Father and Himself can be forgiven, blasphemy against the Holy Spirit can *never* be forgiven in this life or any to come. The one exception is that one learns through experiences in living to forgive oneself; thus, by amending ones life pattern and not repeating serious errors against the Holy Spirit, one becomes contrite in heart and expiates sinful errors.

To question teachings in the search for truth should be considered healthy and desirable, as it is certainly not blasphemous to use our minds which have been created to be *free* and given *choice* by our Supreme Being. This is the *Enlightened Age* in which we who *think* must learn to think in terms not only earthly but *cosmically* as well, if we are to unlock the secret of our own celestial nature and tap this infinite potential. To begin without further delay is vitally important, for the time is indeed short.

In his timeless state, John witnessed the events leading up to and including the ultimate fate of this earth and its inhabitants. For example, "A hail of fire and blood cast upon the earth, and a third part of the trees and green grass burnt up." (Rev. 8:7) We in the present day can still vividly recall the recent wars in Southeast Asia and the programs of vast and irreparable defoliation carried out there by the United States. We saw the massive eruption of the volcanic island of Krakatoa during the latter part of the 19th century which wiped the entire mountain and its island from the face of the earth. The resulting tidal wave, so huge that it circumnavigated the globe, carried shipping and coastal habitations before it. Thousands of lives were lost, or in John's own words, "A great mountain, burning with fire, cast into the sea. And the third part of the sea became blood. A third part of the creatures of the sea die, and a third part of the ships were destroyed." (Rev. 8:8-9).

What of the "great star falling from the heaven, burning as it were a lamp?" John says that "it fell on a third part of the rivers and fountains of water. The name of the star was *Wormwood*, and the waters became poisonous. Many die because the waters were made bitter." (Rev. 8:10-11) The description could have been a veiled reference to the United States Skylab which fell back to earth, although it was non-nuclear. The Russian space station *Soyuz*, which crashed earlier, was fitted with a nuclear power plant. However, based upon facts, this would *not* fit the description given centuries earlier by John. Scientists have already catalogued as "SS433," a mysterious and vivid light object, two thousand times brighter than our sun and emitting variegating colors, and traveling at one-fourth the speed of light. It has already entered the Milky Way galaxy and is now approaching our solar system! Astronomers are completely baffled by the object, and one American scientist is on record as saying, "We've *never* seen anything like it before. Nothing even comes close!" (Authors note: Could this be Sitchin's "nebiru?")

"I saw horses in the vision," the Patmos seer continues. "Their heads were as the heads of lions, and from their mouths issued fire and brimstone; by these were a third part of men killed. Their power is in their mouths and their tails. For their tails were like serpents, and with them they do hurt." (Rev. 9:17-19). A curious passage, difficult to interpret, unless what John saw, but lacked adequate descriptive words to convey, were *modern tanks with revolving turrets and long protruding guns blazing!*

A Dictator Rises

In Chapter 13:1 of Revelations, we find a symbolic reference to a GREAT BEAST which rises out of the sea. It has seven heads and ten horns.

> "Upon its horns, ten crowns, and upon its heads the name of blasphemy. And I saw one of his heads wounded unto death, and his deadly wound was healed. And all the world wondered after the Beast. And worshipped him saying, 'Who is like unto the Beast? Who is able to make war with him?' And there was given unto him a mouth speaking great things and blasphemies, and power was given unto him to continue forty and two months. It was given unto him to make war with the Saints and overcome them, and power was given him over all kindreds and tongues and nations. And all that dwell upon

138

the earth shall worship him, whose names are not written in the Book of Life of the Lamb (the Christus) slain from the foundation of the world" (Rev. 13:1-8). (Authors note: The above refers to League of Nations and rise of Germany once again under Adolf Hitler!)

Further on, in Chapter 17, this creature appears again, "scarlet colored, full of names of blasphemy." Upon its back rides a woman "arrayed in purple and scarlet colors, decked with gold and precious stones; in her hand a cup full of abominations and filthiness." She represents the spirit of absolute materialism and sensuality which dominates the western or modern part of our world in these last days; the antithesis of everything godly and spiritual. The disturbing implication which now springs to mind as we read further is the following:

"Here is the mind which hath wisdom. The seven heads are seven mountains on which the woman sits."

The city of *Rome* is built on *Seven Hills* (the Palatine Hills, including Mount Fiesole which is volcanic in origin).

"There are seven kings. Five are fallen, the other is, and the other is not yet come."

The EEC (European Economic Community, or European Common Market) began with *seven members.*

"The ten horns which thou sawest are then kings who have received no kingdom as yet, but received power as kings one hour with the Beast...these have but one mind, and shall give their strength and power unto the Beast .... for God has put it into their hearts to fulfill His will and agree to give their

139

kingdoms unto the Beast until the word of God be fulfilled." (Rev. 17:12-17).

When the nation of Greece became the newest member of EEC in January of 1982, it then became *Ten Nations or Members!*

It becomes clear that these passages refer to the European Community Alliance. We have seen that the term "Beast" refers to one entity, a *dictator* whose rule becomes absolute over all and persists for forty-two terrible months.

The *Anti-Christ* - how does he establish his rule? How are we to differentiate between him and several other dictators or manipulators who have appeared over these last years upon the world scene? Revelations, Chapter 13, answers both of these questions.

> "I beheld another beast coming out of the earth. He had two horns like a lamb, but spake as a dragon. He exerciseth all power of the first Beast before him, and causeth the earth and them which dwell therein to worship the first Beast whose deadly tail was healed" (13:11-12).

> "And he causeth all, both small and great, rich and poor, free or bond, to receive a mark on their right hand or in their forehead. And that no man may buy or sell, save that he hath the mark or number of the Beast, or the number of his name. Here is wisdom. Let him who hath understanding count the number of the Beast, for it is the number of a man, and his number is six hundred threescore and six." (13:16-18)

The once current five-Deutchmark German banknote depicts on its right-hand side a woman carried upon the back of a horned and winged animal resembling a bull. In her upraised hand she carries a vessel from which brilliant rays stream out in all directions like the rays of the sun. Clearly, the "Beast out of the earth" is closely connected with the European Monetary system, and Germany is surely the country (one of the "ten heads") which was fatally wounded in the last war (World War II), only to make a miraculous recovery and go on to become the economic envy of the world!

> "After all these things," John continues, "I
> saw an angel come down from heaven having
> great power, and the earth was lightened with
> his glory. He cries with a strong voice, saying
> 'Babylon the great is fallen, is fallen. For all
> nations, the kings of the earth, the merchants,
> are waxed rich through the abundance of her
> delicacies.' And I heard another voice out of
> heaven, saying, 'Come out of her, my people,
> that ye be not partakers of her transgressions
> and receive not of her plagues'" (Rev. 18:1-
> on)

It soon becomes clear that the name *Babylon* refers to the EEC Bloc and now European Union. And from the last message alone it is obvious that the whole corrupt and materialistic system on which the community is based is an offense to the Lord, this all-powerful Being whose messengers are watching us of earth so closely from the dimensions beyond, their craft seen daily, hourly, in the skies all over the world. Those of us who are faithful to the Christus—by whatever name we call Him—are being warned to have nothing to do with this system. It is evil, and would soon be destroyed. It is a *monetary system*, plain and simple, by which the *Anti-Christ* will seek to enslave, body and soul, the peoples of the world. (Read all of Revelations 13 with great care).

The idea behind the *European Monetary System* is that the major currencies of the EEC shall have a fixed relationship to each other with a central fund modeled upon the International Monetary Fund. This would provide finance for currencies under pressure to insure that they are not forced to devalue. The inevitable outcome of this policy will be to compel other member countries to pursue the same economic strategy, and eventually the EMS (European Monetary System) will propose a common currency for the whole community. (Authors note: Euro-dollar). The way would then be wide open for the financial system indicated in Chapter 13 of Revelations. All people within the Community, whatever their status or income group, would be obliged to comply. Any threat to withdraw the vital number would, in itself, ensure a minimum number of dissenters, and the potential for abuse of every kind is incalculable.

The Number of the Beast

In May, 1975 it was announced from Brussels by Dr. Hendrick Elderman, Chief Analyst for the Common Market Confederacy, that a computerized restoration plan was being formulated to deal with the aftermath of a world-wide crisis. A top-level meeting was held by advisors, scientists and EEC financier personnel. At that meeting Dr. Elderman introduced a HUGE COMPUTER, so big in fact, that it takes up no less than three entire floors of the Market Headquarters Administrative Building. The very latest showplace of modern technology, the computer is an entirely self-programming unit with more than 100 sensing input sources. In other words, it is capable of thinking, reasoning, and making decisions without the benefit of human help. It has been nicknamed by the team who designed and built it - **THE BEAST!**

How would it work? The number, says Dr. Elderman, would be invisibly and painlessly tattooed by a laser onto the forehead or the back of the hand! He suggests that by the use of three six-digital units, the entire population of the world could be issued with a working credit number.

In case it has escaped the reader's notice "six-hundred threescore and six" (666) comes into this very category. Remember also, that details of this plan only came to light in the year 1975. How much progress has transpired since this time is a matter open only to our understanding. However, we do know that in "shopping" a *digital number* is now used in most large markets (at least in the United States). The use of *digital numbers* has now been going on since the year 1971 internationally.

The "Beast" is also linked with a vast computer network in the United States. This too may be significant considering the present economic state of this country. Even a blind man can see from the warning formerly given from Sheik Yamani of OPEC (oil cartel), that unless the West finds an alternative energy source soon in place of oil, the results will be disastrous. We are standing upon the threshold of world recession in which the "Beast" will come into his own! We may actually now be in just such a position.

Make no mistake! There are going to be many people who recognize in this evil system the fulfillment of the biblical prophecy. Many will refuse to comply and great physical hardship and spiritual persecution will result. This, too, the Book of Revelation makes abundantly clear. It is the inevitable collision of a head-on battle between materialism and spirituality whenever the individual consciously defies the vast vested interests which seek to sweep aside Divine Law. It is an essential part of that confrontation between the Children of Light and the Children of Darkness (as an example of the Sons of One versus the Sons of Belial, or Baal). It is happening now! It will be on the increase in the near future. *BE WARNED! BE PREPARED!*

What Should We Do?

What can we, the Children of Light, do in order to survive until the prophecies are fulfilled - the Christus returns and the earth is made new?

First of all, we must search our own hearts in the light of this new knowledge and decide exactly what our priorities are. Once our decision is made there will be no going back, and it cannot long be postponed, for time is short. The "Beast" and its world-wide plan will have much to do with the coming time period, and will no doubt reveal itself as a result of international affairs. It will soon also become apparent that the mass numbering of peoples has begun and will continue to affect and infect every individual in the western part of the world. Would one accept or refuse to be numbered? This is a matter for each individual to decide. Let us now study in detail what the result of either course may mean.

If we were to accept the number it would mean renunciation of the spiritual path totally. There is no way to cushion the harshness of this reality for there is NO compromise with evil. For to accept willingly is to relinquish ones personal freedom and identity as well as the freedom of choice and dissent, in exchange for material comforts, and being supported financially by the system in event of unemployment, illness, etc. This also does not mean necessarily that ones standard of living will improve as the system itself becomes more powerful and affluent. The rich will continue to get rich at the expense of the poor, who will either remain poor or become more destitute, as seemingly it has always been in western society. Only the "haves" stand to gain as much from the "Beast" as they will lose.

To refuse the "number" would be to court disaster! Have no illusions about that! Therefore, to accept or reject would literally be a choice between physical life, or quite probably physical death by reason of deprivation, resulting in starvation. In the event of a really devastating world upheaval, democracy and law and order may break down fully or in part, meaning that dissenters may be imprisoned, coerced, subjected to force, or simply left to starve. Panic stricken societies are violent societies. In any event, the numberless person will officially cease to exist! Not only will he or she be *unable* to buy or sell, but there will be *no* means by which to pay ones bills, send letters, maintain a telephone, travel, give or receive gifts, legacies, money or property, or to provide for self or a dependent. Even those who would imagine themselves to be self-sufficient will still be in need of money or capital of some type to purchase seeds, tools, equipment and the basic materials with which to provide themselves with shelter, clothing, heat and medical aid. Ponder deeply upon the implications of this course of action, for there are many.

It is *vital for the survival of the enlightened peoples everywhere* that existing self-sufficient communities step up their efforts to become *totally* rather than partially self-sufficient, and as far as possible, to *amalgamate* with each other, bearing in mind the old adage that *UNITY IS STRENGTH!* The same applies to all Light Centers - they should make themselves as widely known as possible. Both may be called upon when the time comes to offer comfort, shelter, and spiritual guidance to vast numbers of lost and frightened people from all walks of life, many of whom will have lost faith in their own clergy at that time. Enlightened people still living in the cities should make an urgent effort to change their place of abode to one where the cooperation and encouragement of like minds is readily accessible. We must stress again that for the numberless (those who have refused to bow to the demand that they must be numbered in order to carry on life as usual), there will be *no* means of travel other than by foot and *no* means of communication other than by word of mouth. Even motorbikes break down and parts for replacement have to be purchased.

Already the *Space Intelligence* have guided many of us out of the cities to the more accessible rural areas in readiness for the final confrontation between GOOD and EVIL, when the CHRISTUS WILL RETURN TO CLAIM HIS OWN. Soon, with the oil resources dwindling and prices rocketing, the inevitable decline in private motor transport will begin. City-based commuters who find it expedient to live nearer to their place of employment will gradually begin the exodus back to the towns and cities.

145

With the resultant decline in the country property values, more and more self-sufficient people will move out to the rural areas, towns and farms, particularly those areas close to more spiritual and sacred places. All of these points are in accordance with the plans of the *Space Intelligence*. It is somewhat difficult for *them* when they must penetrate the pollution of our skies and the overcrowded conditions of our cities, so full of poisonous fumes, noise and foul vibrations. Out in the relatively quiet, clean air of the rural country, the Master's children can more easily be contacted "in person" or "telepathically" marked with the seal of His acceptance and eventually removed. Revelations assures us that the earth shall not be harmed until the "angels" have *sealed*, for purposes of identification, those 144,000 highly evolved incarnates who have been chosen as leaders and restorers of the PLAN who will be returned to the changed earth after the so-called holocaust has passed. This holy *seal* is probably being applied through several of applicable choices left to the *Space Intelligence* and could very possibly be applied during times of sleep (Rev. 7:1-4).

This is the time to gather together, to cling together in the face of events which are soon to come. It is time to give our friends and loved ones that extra time, attention and care which we can so easily spare if we really try. We must pray constantly for those whose eyes are not yet fully opened to what is taking place. The Messengers wait, invisible but ever present, to learn the names of those for whom we intercede!

It is time to work upon our spiritual evolvement. We should pay particular attention to those little things which keep us mired in a low vibrational level. We have need to raise our vibrations a little every day to a degree where the change from matter to energy, when it comes, will be instantaneous and delightful. Not the passing of the Spirit from the body - that will come at a later date - but the actual transmutation of the material substance of ones body to a higher vibratory rate to match that of the "new earth" which is to be our inheritance (Rev. 21). We must become conscious, willing and active participants with the *Space Intelligence* in helping to establish the *Age of Truth.* Those of us who do refuse the "number" and also refuse to compromise our spiritual morality together with the system may well lose our lives - but we will be spiritually sustained. On the other hand, in our new condition, we may no longer need material sustenance at all to truly live! The Christus has promised that for our sakes, the DAYS OF TRIBULATION WILL BE CUT SHORT. In such circumstances, the true Children of Light will receive proper protection.

Even if we are called upon in the short term to suffer the extremes of deprivation, undergo abuse, ridicule, and be subjected to every type of injustice - remember that so was the Master Christus. No matter by what name we might call Him—Krishna, Osiris, Massau'u, Jesus—we are His and He is ours forever. Nothing and nobody will ever separate Him from us except by our own self-ego. The cruelty of this world will never again touch us with its immoral pollution and many will listen. But every day, every hour, is precious from now until this Tribulation shall be lifted from the world!

According to Revelations and other prophetical works in the Holy Bible, to our Creator and His son the Christus, the EEC and European Union (New World Order) is the ultimate abominations of callous materialistic greed. Its industries strip the earth of her resources for the benefit of an affluent minority who grow rich and fat while two-thirds of the earth's population starve. While babies wither and die at their mothers' empty breasts, it permits vast stores of milk and huge deposits of food to be wantonly destroyed because it cannot be sold for a high enough profit - unless, of course, it is politically expedient to do so! It feeds upon the merciless, darker exploitation of everything that brotherhood, compassion and charity are supposed to be about among those dwelling on earth. As its powers increase, exploitation and injustice will increase accordingly, and what we have come to enjoy as democracy will decline and disappear for a period of time.

The man or woman who willingly accepts the "number of the Beast" does so in full accordance with the law of free choice. The Creator did not program us to be mindless automatons, to always choose *good* rather than *evil*. He wants our loyalty, but not at that high a price. But the individual who turns against the Father of Lights to worship the "Beast" of materialism and his "Mark," aligns himself/herself with that terrible dark spirit personified by a people in whom the divine spark will have been extinguished. It appears that the new emerging trinity will be *vanity, wealth and power!*

But what will become of those who do accept the "Number of the Beast?"

> "If any man shall worship the Beast and his image, the same shall drink of the fury of God, poured out without mixture into the cup of His indignation. He shall be tormented with fire in the presence of the Holy Angels and of the Lamb (Christus). They shall have no rest day or night, who worship the Beast and receive the mark of his name." (Rev. 14:10-11)

It is vitally important to interpret the last message with the *utmost care*. Some Christian sects believe that it refers to the physical torment of those referred to in an equally physical hell of flames and fire. Yet, the verse states plainly that the punishment takes place before the Christus and His angels, who are dwellers of the parallel world (etheric or spiritual) realms. It follows then, that if the "torment" cannot be of the physical body, it must be of the mind, which in this case, has abandoned itself to materialism, sensuality, and every kind of self-indulgence. Imagine then the horror and despair of that mind which finds its physical instrument destroyed unto death, and without the

148

material body it can no longer enjoy and participate in its former earthly pleasures upon which its whole purpose has been centered. Being unfit for the spiritual dimensions, it cannot rise unto the Light until it has totally surrendered unto God, the Father of Light! It must, therefore, remain trapped by its own actions in the insane and illusory place of a lower level with the earth's materiality as its background, where desire is ever present and satisfaction can never be found. There it must stay, overcome by regret and self-disgust until freed by its own repentance and a desire to make amends and atone for its previous actions. This is the Law of Cause and Effect that some refer to as *karma*, from which none of us is exempt.

The fate of the EEC or European Union described at length in Revelations, Chapter 18, makes somber reading. The last verse refers explicitly to the persecution and slaughter of dissenters within the system itself, and the fate of helpless millions in other lands and nations whose lives are now, or will soon become impoverished by it. These will, of course, also include multitudes of the Third World nations—those who become pawns in the battle between great powers. They will be mown down by armaments manufactured in rich nations, poisoned by drugs and chemicals deemed too dangerous to be used in the Western nations, but sold off callously to poorer nations for the sake of increased profit. Included will be those whose resources are stolen, and whose cultures are being destroyed for the sake of feeding the voracious appetites of Western industry.

But the Christus is NOT sleeping! He who is LOVE is watching, waiting and biding His time. His signs are seen daily, hourly in the skies all over this fearful and bullied world. His Holy "messengers" already walk the earth in secret among us, often in bodies resembling flesh and bone like our own, encouraging, sustaining, and preparing His loved ones.

Remember His words, "Hold fast to that which you have, so that no man shall take your crown." Hold fast to the knowledge that to all evil there is an end, and that end is at last in sight. All things shall be made new; the old sorrows shall pass away and God will wipe away all tears from your eyes.

SO BE STRONG! BE PREPARED!
KEEP YOUR FACE TOWARD THE EAST!

CHAPTER TWELVE
TOWARD THE FUTURE

Through our *extraterrestrial source*, this book has explored the relationship between mythology, prophecy, and UFOs throughout our planet's history. Now we must ask the question: "Have we come to the period in the affairs of man when what had been prophesied is now upon us?" Many are aware that we live in a time when earthquakes happen with ever increasing intensity. Exploding volcanoes that have lain dormant for centuries are blackening our skies. Floods and high velocity wind storms wreak havoc on our population in increasing numbers; hate, prejudice and militant factions run rampant; and... now more than ever, UFOs and their occupants are witnessed daily by thousands of people all over the world.

We have now had over 50 years of what alleges to be visitation by "objects unknown" flying through the skies of earth, and also many claims of physical contact with the beings inhabiting these strange craft. We have been told that this is a time for great and potentially enlightening change in the imperceptible senses within mankind. It also appears that we are fast approaching spiritual insight into Biblical prophecy, and those prophecies which have come into great importance and prominence by Native Americans.

The Banner – A gift to the Hopi

It was in October of 1994 that a very close friend of mine decided to come for a visit. Tsering, who is of Tibetan birth, wished to present a Tibetan Banner to be displayed within the Hopi Council Chambers on their reservation in northern Arizona. I contacted my friend, Sakina Blue Star, who was a good friend of the then Council member, Thomas Banyacaya. I had met with Mr. Banyacaya in Santa Barbara, California at an earlier time and was privileged to speak with him regarding Native American prophecy.

151

Tsering, his mother Dorje, and several members of my own family departed for the Hopi Reservation. Within several hours, we arrived at the home of the honorable Council member, Mr. Banyacaya. We were graciously greeted by him and his wife as they bid us to seat ourselves and share some food on the patio. We then began to discuss the reason that our Tibetan friend had traveled so far from his home in northern California.

Tsering explained that he had come to present a Banner to the Hopi. If accepted, this Banner would be placed within the Hopi Council Chamber. We were startled when Mr. Banyacaya stated, "Oh, you are one of the Southern People that would one day come and bring us something to unite us together." Then giving his blessing to Tsering, Mr. Banyacaya permitted us, under the guidance of Sakina Blue Star, to travel to the home of "Grandfather Martin," a Hopi Elder, where the gift of the Banner was presented. We later learned that the Banner had indeed been placed upon the east wall of the Council Chamber (Kiva) between two other sacred Hopi objects.

I spoke to Tsering in detail as to the meaning of the Banner he had presented to the Hopi. I was surprised and very excited upon learning that the Banner's meaning had to do with the Kalachakra or Wheel of Fire, which deals with "'Revelation and Truth." Immediately, I recognized and grasped its significance. While living in California years ago, I had come into contact with a gentleman who had in his possession an object referred to as a "Brass Horse." Evidently, this "Brass Horse" had been smuggled out of Tibet before being overrun by the Chinese Communists. The Horse had several identifying symbols. One was a "plate" between its ears that portrayed a "triangle;" another was a "flayed man" draped over the saddle. In the middle of the saddle was an indented hole into which was placed a brass "flame" with blue and red colors about its inner rim and a six-pointed star within it. There were other identifying symbols; however, the loose brass plate beneath the horse intrigued us most. Perhaps there was something contained therein. We *very carefully* opened the "waxed-in" brass plate, and were startled to discover somewhat eroded but tightly rolled rice paper "scrolls" wrapped in silk. We further discovered that these scrolls were ancient Tibetan "script" in both black and red ink, which was used at that time. Our research revealed that the Horse was referred to as "The Fiery Steed Carrying the Flaming Pearl of Truth and Revelation!" To this day, there has been no further translation of these "scripts." Perhaps we had been carefully led to discover and uncover the meaning of "Revelation and Truth."

Unbeknownst to Tsering at the time, by this act of presenting the "Banner" to the Hopi nation, he became "One of the Southern People," opening the door for the rest of the prophecies to take place. Tsering was surprised to learn what had been accomplished by this most innocent gesture; however, I am sure that he had been "led" by much "Higher Sources" to carry it out.

Kachina Deities

There have been other wondrous events taking place on the Hopi-Dineh (Navajo) Reservation. Many thousands of Native Americans have by now traveled to the area called Rocky Ridge in the Big Mountain locale to witness and speak with the women who experienced the following on the morning of May 3, 1995.

Irene Yazzie had not spoken for several months because of a stroke. But this morning, she turned to her daughter to tell her that someone was coming to their home near Big Mountain north of Flagstaff. About noon, the two heard a loud noise outside, followed by someone knocking. Opening the door, they encountered two tall, elderly men who appeared to be Native American. One of the men told them not to be afraid; they were two of the more than one hundred Dineh Kachina deities who assist in all aspects of Dineh life. They had appeared before Irene and her daughter to ask why the deities no longer were receiving prayers from the people. They warned that if the Dineh continued to forsake Tribal traditions, they were to face grave danger in the future. The Dineh deities would not be able to help. Seconds later, the men vanished, leaving only footprints and a sprinkling of corn pollen upon their hearth. (Traditional Dineh sprinkle or scatter this corn pollen during prayers).

Research from a former historian for the Tribe revealed that such deities appeared during the 1930's and 1950's. In each case, the deity had appeared to elderly Dineh women during a time of drought.

Other Significant Events

In June of 1995 the Australian Aboriginal "Dream Dancers" from its Outback region had long wanted to come to the United States and participate with the Native Americans in Arizona. They finally got their wish. The President of the Dineh nation, Albert Hale, said in a memo, "This is a significant event to Navajo (Dineh) people everywhere. These Aboriginal Native people, who are ancient descendants by all historical records, maintain their sacred dances and ceremonial rites. They are one of the races of the 'Southern People.'"

After arriving in the United States, they gathered with the Piman, Papago, Yavapai, Hopi and Dineh (Navajo) on the Maricopa-Pima Reservation and carried out their sacred dances.

Shortly after this event, Tibetan monks from the Drepung-Loseling Monastery in the Himalayas came to Arizona to carry out a week-long fair in Flagstaff. When the fair ended, these "Southern People" traveled to the Hopi-Dineh Reservation and carried out ceremonies and sacred dances in August, 1995. We can now certainly say that the Northern and Southern people are UNITED ONCE MORE!

It wasn't long before several more ancient prophecies came to pass. Could it be that our present Age and Cycle is that which was told in ancient times to Native Americans of Mayan and Aztec descent? On March 21, 1997, thousands

154

of worshippers prayed amid clouds of Copal incense and pounding drums at the Pyramid of The Sun (Teotihuacan) in the ancient dead city of the Aztecan people Tenochtitlan. "Hail Teotihuacan; Hail The Sun," they chanted, as others clutched quartz stones and Indian men danced wildly in their costumes of feathered headdresses.

"The magical world still survives in Mexico, and it is felt on days such as this," states Homero Aridji, a Mexican author, who says it is legend that our current and "Fifth Sun" was created in Teotihuacan.

Following upon that event, several thousand Native American children began returning to their reservations after finding that they had been taken by government social workers when they were babies. Their parents were told they would be unable to care for them, so they were to be placed with "foster families." These former foster children had now discovered that they were of Native Tribal people instead of what they had formerly been led to believe.

Yellow Star—White Buffalo

Recently, Mr. Robert Morning Sky, who is both Hopi and Apache, said in newspaper reports that the recent "Hale-Bopp Comet" might be the legendary "Yellow Star" or an ancient "sign of the end of time" that Hopi Elders have been expecting for centuries. He states that if Hale-Bopp isn't the "Star" that the Hopi's and others have been talking about, its appearance certainly fits into the prophecy. Robert Morning Sky had appeared on a radio program broadcast in Gallup, New Mexico, which is heard throughout the Dineh Reservation. He told his version of the "Hale-Bopp," a comet that returns after a 4,000 year absence. He further stated that the "end of time" prophecy, one of the best known in Hopi tradition, tells the story of an older brother who takes a sacred stone to the "rising sun." When he arrives at his destination, a "White Star in the sky" signals his return to Hopi Land in seven seasons. According to Morning Star, if a "season" is the designation for a year, then the "end of time"

155

prophesy would come in 2004 A.D. The Aztecs also predicted that the realization of this prophecy would come about in May of 2004. Of course, if a "season" turns out to be longer than a year, we have the Mayan prophesy which says that the last day of the earth as we know it will be on December 21, 2012.

There are reasons why the Hopi prophecies should be taken seriously. The "Star" in their prophecy can be traced to the birth of a rare white buffalo on August 20, 1994, on a Janesville, Wisconsin farm. (Recently, we have been informed that the owners of this famous buffalo have relocated to Flagstaff, Arizona). This event attracted the attention of hundreds of Native American spiritual leaders who felt the birth signaled major changes about to occur. This buffalo has now turned the four colors said to be associated with the prophecy. According to Morning Sky, an omen such as this must have a "twin" or similar event of a sacred type that occurs close in time. When a second white buffalo was born in May of 1995, the "commencement of the prophecy" was confirmed. Morning Sky states that the two comets, "Hyakutake" in 1996 and the "Hale-Bopp" comet in 1997, are the same as the two white buffalo births.

Strange Writing and the Phenomenon of "Crop Circles"

While channeling information from my *source* in the 1950's, I was given some form of pictographic writing. Since I had no idea at the time what the writing meant, I put it away in a safe place. Shortly after I received this "writing," I attended a UFO conference in Las Vegas where Carl Van Vlierden, author of *The Twelve Planets Speak* was giving a lecture. I took the strange writing with me. During his lecture, Mr. Van Vlierden showed a slide of what appeared to be the IDENTICAL PICTOGRAPHIC LANGUAGE that I had in my possession! I was flabbergasted! I spoke with Van Vlierden after his lecture and he examined the writing. He concurred there was no doubt that I was in touch with the *same beings* as those in

Van Vlierden's South African group. He also informed me that they had received their information in the same manner as myself!

It has been concluded that these "writings" may depict the original "tongue" spoken by those who were inhabiting or visiting planet earth prior to or during the period of the legendary lost continent of Atlantis prior to 10,000 B.C. According to my *source,* this tongue was known as "Solex Mal," or "Solar Mother Tongue" before its demise during the wars of the Tigris-Euphrates Valley (Iraq-Iran), or the archeological period of the "Towers of Babel," and the destruction of the two Sumerian cities of Mohenyo-Daro and Harrapa.

The *Space Intelligence* has further informed me that these strange petroglyphs are indeed very ancient and are related to what is now happening worldwide with the phenomenon of "Crop Circles." My source states that approximately one fourth of crop circles are man made, and the remainder due to magnetic factors which create pictograph language related to the "plain of Nazca" (Peru). Some of these crop circle pictographs signify various locations in the heavens where intelligent life may be found; some signify equations and spiritual symbolism relating to the formation of other civilizations presently existing upon other planets. Found within some of the pictographs is a form of code relaying information about our past, present and future, and may also refer to the populace dwelling in a given location. The country of Great Britain has certainly seen its share of crop circles in recent years. According to my *source,* Great Britain is one of the oldest vestiges of the former Atlantean civilization still above the ocean waters. The people of this country relate to many other races who had migrated since ancient times throughout our world. There have been, as well, other locations around the world where *Space Intelligence* have left these crop circle "signs" for our inquiry and investigation. However, it is disappointing that those upon our planet who wish to foster both misunderstanding and confusion by creating "false" crop circles have indeed created doubt in the minds of many. Because of this, the *Space Intelligence* may seriously consider no further explanation of the extraterrestrial means that create such "signs." However, the recent "basket weave" crop circle that appeared in Great Britain was so intricate in its design and formation that those who still exhibit doubt and skepticism as to its origin and creativity would find great difficulty in recreating it. I have been informed that it is an ancient design and format of our Native Americans and is a representation of our world and its intelligence.

It is interesting to note that Sedona, Arizona is a very ancient ceremonial site of the original Sinagua people who inhabited the Verde Valley up until approximately 1100 A.D. Since this makes the area somewhat sacred to the Native people, all those who presently dwell in this region would necessarily come under a great spiritual energy. Perhaps it would then stand to reason that this entire region would also be visited by inhabitants of other worlds beyond our own who arrive here via spaceships. The "signs" and photographs that have been discovered in this region allege to be extraterrestrial in origin, and may very well be "other worldly." It is time that we give very careful consideration to the relationship between mythology, prophecy and our visitors from space. Perhaps our "crop circles" tell the story.

Do the "Heavenly Hosts" still Speak?

Should we only look to the past for the voice of the Heavenly Hosts? Or is it possible that *they* are alive and well and still sending us universal teachings and messages? I believe they are. The following was communicated to me by my own *source—Space Intelligence beings* whom I consider "Heavenly Hosts." Their wish is that this information will be helpful in awakening those upon planet earth who would hear:

Might this be left with you to think upon!

158

Shall you of the earth allow destruction once again? Shall you say to the technologists who may have gone astray, along with leaderships in nations having become corrupted by their mistaken use of power: "Must we once again allow darkness to engulf our world and further destroy what magnificent works have been constructed upon our surface?"

Even now the footprints of darkness appear again upon the panoply of history presently upon your planet! One would give warning that if you understand that all this CAN come upon you, and yet stand idle and do nothing to aid in its prevention, then you shall be the decider of the results. However, if you remember that the Lord God is your SHIELD and BUCKLER, through spiritual strength, one can be effectual in bringing about a change for constructive purpose in your fellow human being or environment. Therefore, you shall have moved toward a harmonious result in the "Covenant of the Rainbow" remaining with the people of earth. This Covenant was so long ago given by Almighty God, Father of Lights, to His children; that His children's children and their children's children shall live out their days in the Love, Light and Peace which the Lord of Lights shall bestow upon all of you. When one understands that ALL IS ONE, then they are true teachers of enlightenment.

In order to prepare for the time ahead, you would be wise to gain insight into your own spiritual nature, making use of this insight in your everyday lives. Humans are faced with such difficulties as misinterpretation, misunderstanding, anger and resentment— some of what is referred to as the seven deadly errors (sins) of your civilization. By working to overcome these errors, you learn to rise above that of the lower nature and are more able to be of service to your fellow man, although at times they may display or vent their own resentment or anger. Every great master that has been sent to earth has come to teach you this: Being of service to ones fellow man is the greatest honor that can be bestowed upon each of you. It has been said, "If one builds his Temple upon a rock, it should withstand the roaring sea."

Therefore, manifest this service to others upon your world's dimension, and know that you can project your mental processes into higher spiritual realms in order to gain knowledge, information and encouragement to sustain you on your path.

Now, dear ones, we are leaving the plane of your existence.

Adonai, vasu barragas…
Hail God…Farewell, Good Brothers.

Bibliography

Ancient Near Eastern Texts relating to The Old Testament, edited by J. B. Pritchard Princeton University Press.

Childress, David. *Vimana Aircraft of Ancient India and Atlantis,* Kempton, IL: Adventures Unlimited Press, 1957.

Corso, Philip J. *The Day After Roswell,* New York: Pocketbooks, 1997.

Dowding, (British Air Chief Marshall). BUFORA, Flying Saucer Review: approx. 1952-1957.

Drake, W. R. (Berossus, Babylonian historian). *Gods or Spacemen,* Amherst Press, 1964.

Fenoglio, Alberto. From the Magazine Clypeus, *Ur, Assur and Babylon,* by H. Schmoekel, Italy: Anno. III, N.2

Holy Bible, King James Edition – abridged

Keyhoe, Donald. *Aliens From Space: The Real Story of Unidentified Flying Objects,* Garden City, NY: Doubleday, 1973.

Khem (Egypt) Ancient papyrus scribed by the priests: Annuals of the House of Life.

Koenig, Herr. *9 JAHRE IRAK,* (iron rods encased in copper cylinders in ancient Babylon), Austria, 1940.

Manuscript from the Prehistoric Past; (from the Bhagadvatham).

Nidle, Sheldon "You Are Becoming A Galactic Human" S. E. E. Publishing Co., Santa Clara, Calif., 1994.

Mahabharata and Parvas, Drona Parvas (ancient text) pages 317-340.

Roberts, Henry. *The Complete Prophecies of Nostradamus*, Nostradamus, Inc., Citadel Press, 1949.

Sitchin, Zecharia. *The Twelfth Planet,* New York: Stein and Day, 1976.

Tange, Yosiyuki. The Cosmic Brotherhood Association magazine published in Japan, 1950's to 1970's. No longer in publication.

Vallee, Jacques. *Challenge To Science---The UFO Enigma: The Psychic Solution,*" Chicago, Henry Regenery, 1966. London,

Walton, Bruce, (Source): Credit to Morris E. Opler. *American Folklore Society,* New York: G. E. Stechert and Co.